Intercultural Church

Intercultural Church

A Biblical Vision for an Age of Migration

Safwat Marzouk

Fortress Press
Minneapolis

INTERCULTURAL CHURCH
A Biblical Vision for an Age of Migration

We gratefully acknowledge that the table liturgy entitled "Gathered around
the Table" was developed by Alan and Eleanor Kreider, and permission has
been granted to use it in this book.

Hymns in "Gathered around the Table" are used by permission of GIA
Publications, Inc., 7404 S. Mason Ave., Chicago, IL 60638, www.giamusic
.com, 800.442.1358, and Hope Publishing Company. See the full copyright
and reprint permission lines at the bottom each hymn.

Cover image: Old Woman with child trailing refugees. IStock Images /
xochicalco.
Cover Design: Alisha Lofgren

Print ISBN: 978-1-5064-3346-2
ebook ISBN: 978-1-5064-3821-4

The paper used in this publication meets the minimum requirements of
American National Standard for Information Sciences—Permanence of
Paper for Printed Library Materials, ANSI Z329, 48-1984.

Manufactured in the U.S.A.

For Calista and Julian
and many like them
who live in liminal spaces between cultures

CONTENTS

INTRODUCTION

In the wake of recent waves of migration and movements of refugees, the church is confronted with a challenge and offered an opportunity. In addition to its advocacy work on behalf of the undocumented, asylum seekers, and refugees, the church is faced with the challenge of what it means to be a church in light of the ever-growing diversity of the population of our society. In other words, as important as it is for Christian and non-Christian activists to work toward welcoming the stranger and the migrant, the question remains: What has the community done to integrate the migrant and the stranger so they become part of the society?

The church may ask a related question: As the church musters biblical resources to advocate for welcoming the refugee and the migrant, what has the church done to make these migrants part of the body of Christ? Do migrants end up living in segregated communities, separated from one another and from the dominant culture? Are they expected to give up their culture, language, habits, and customs and be assimilated into the mainstream culture, so they feel like they fit in the society to which they have migrated? Are churches willing to change their worship, leadership, and ministry in order to embrace the diverse communities that are present in their neighborhoods?

At the same time, other questions can be raised concerning migrant communities: Are these communities isolating themselves from the surrounding society and churches in order to maintain their cultural identity? Or do they feel like they have nothing to offer and should merely work to become like the dominant culture in order to fit in? Reflecting on these questions is an important starting point toward thinking about what God is calling the church to be in light of the recent waves of migration. Reflecting on these questions will put the church on the edge of the hard and challenging process of change, but such reflection holds great promise for the church and for the world.

Migration does not just bring to the fore the challenge of societal change; migration brings with it an opportunity to rediscover what it means to be a diverse human society and a diverse body of Christ. The opportunity that migration holds is not simply about filling the growing vacancy in church pews with migrant members who will follow a particular brand of theology or worship. Rather, migration holds the possibility and the promise that the church can rediscover its identity as envisioned in the Bible. This book seeks to invite Christian communities that come from different racial and ethnic backgrounds—both communities that migrated a long time ago

> Migration holds the possibility and the promise that the church can rediscover its identity as envisioned in the Bible.

and recent migrant or refugee communities—to respond to the biblical vision of the church as a diverse faith community.

From its inception, the church was meant to be a diverse community. On the day of the Pentecost, the Holy Spirit inaugurated the church by proclaiming the gospel in a multiplicity of languages. In the eschatological vision of the church in Revelation 4–7, the worshipping community, which offers God and the Lamb praises of glory and honor, comes from many nations, tribes, languages, and peoples. While the church in North America might see migration as an opportunity to serve God's kingdom by showing hospitality to the migrant and the alien, migration offers the church an opportunity to renew itself by rediscovering the biblical vision of the church as a diverse community. This biblical vision views cultural, linguistic, racial, and ethnic differences as gifts from God that can enrich the church's worship, deepen the sense of fellowship in the church, and broaden the church's witness to God's reconciling mission in the world.

A Biblical Vision

This book offers a biblical vision for what it means to be an intercultural church. In the first chapter of this book, I will explain in more detail what I mean by an intercultural church, but in short, an intercultural church is a church that fosters a just diversity, integrates different cultural articulations of faith and worship, and embodies in the world an alternative to the politics of assimilation and segregation. For the most part, our churches across the denominations operate under one of two models. The first is an assimilation model, where a dominant culture is assumed, and all different members must assimilate into this dominant culture. The second is a segregation model, in which the different cultural or ethnic communities end up worshipping separately. I will suggest that the models of assimilation and segregation try to get rid of theological and cultural differences, but the church that fosters an intercultural identity learns how to embrace and celebrate difference, which in turn will enrich its worship and ministry.

What are the biblical foundations for this claim? How would the church get there? The starting point, I will suggest, is that the church is ultimately God's project. While peculiar cultural expressions of faith, worship, and ministry are essential to the life of the church, what remains at the center of the church is God, not a particular culture. The story of Peter and Cornelius in Acts 10 builds on this foundation, claiming that for the church to cross new boundaries and to embrace difference, the members of the church who come from different cultural backgrounds need to recognize that their need for one another is mutual. Further, they need to receive the gifts they can offer each other and must realize that conversion and change are the responsibility of all parties involved in the congregation.

The church's attitude toward migrants and toward the notion of cultural diversity among its members can be transformed through a close reading of the Bible from the perspective of those who were forced to leave their homeland. The second chapter of this book focuses on the observation that the biblical texts of both ancient Israel and the early church were written by authors living in exile and diaspora. Not only that, but the Bible identifies Israel's ancestors as alien residents and sojourners. In the New Testament, this identity is extended to the church. Such an identity is muddied in our contemporary contexts because the texts that were written by exiles and migrants are now read by settled communities and well-established churches. The church can become an intercultural community when those who immigrated a long time ago sit together with recent migrants to discern what it means to read the Bible through the eyes of the displaced. The church also needs to ponder the ethical approaches it should have toward the world, given that God calls the church to be a community of alien residents and sojourners.

If the eschatological vision of the church's worship of God and the Lamb in Revelation 4–7 asserts that the church is to be made up of people who come from different ethnic, tribal, cultural, and linguistic backgrounds, then how should this vision become a reality for the church here and now? How should this vision inspire church members to embrace new practices of worship that emerge from a culture different from their own? How should such a vision challenge the members of the church to worship with others who speak a different language? As the visions of Revelation 4–7 emphasize the diversity of the worshipping community in terms of cultural backgrounds and in terms of the multiplicity of ways to worship God, these visions also give voice to different spiritualities by creating a healthy tension between songs of praise and prayers of lament. Therefore, chapter 3 of this book will make the point that an intercultural church succeeds in reflecting this eschatological vision here and now if it becomes diverse not only in the styles of worship but also in the spiritualities that are integrated in the same worship.

The stories of the Tower of Babel and Pentecost have been a feature of most of the discussions that seek to celebrate cultural and linguistic diversity within the faith community. While recent scholarship affirms cultural and linguistic diversity in the story of the Tower of Babel, one is left wondering whether communication is possible in a multicultural human community in which people speak different languages. How will the different and diverse people communicate with one another? Many scholars have suggested that Pentecost is not a reversal of Babel. While I agree with this position, I will propose in chapter 4 that, unlike Babel, which leaves behind a multicultural community in which communication is lacking, Pentecost transforms the multicultural model into an intercultural model in which communication is possible. An intercultural church where multiple languages exist will need to listen to the call of the Spirit to develop the skills of translation. Translation happens here on two levels. There is a linguistic level, which involves translating songs, prayers, and sermons into multiple languages. And there is a cultural level, in which people learn how to negotiate cultural sameness and difference, appreciate other cultures understand and adapt to them, and exercise discernment and critical thinking about their own culture and other cultures. In such an intercultural church, people will be able to learn and grow together in knowing God, themselves, and one another.

For the members of an intercultural church to know each other's beliefs, language, and culture better, these congregants need to share sacred meals together. The Bible is full of stories in which food and meals have played a significant role in forming a diverse communities. For example, I explore the meal that played an important part in the peace treaty or covenant between Isaac and the Philistines in Genesis 26. Or consider what Paul says about the conflict in the church of Corinth and the church's behavior around meals and the Lord's Supper (1 Corinthians 10–11). Food also plays a role in the hospitality shown to Ruth, the foreigner, and in integrating her into the Israelite community. The discussion in chapter 5 will show that food can play a significant role in deepening the communion between the members of the body of Christ in an intercultural church. Preparing meals to eat with other people who come from different cultures allows people to claim their cultural identity while offering and receiving food, which is so basic and essential to human existence.

The intercultural church is a missional church. I will explain in chapter 6 how the intercultural church can practice its witness to God's reconciling mission in the world in three different ways. First, an intercultural church can be a place of offering pastoral care for those who experience fear and anxiety because the world they have known is changing around them. It can reach out to those who have been uprooted from their soil and are now looking to extend their roots in a new land. Second, migrants are not simply seeking to receive help from the host community; migrants also have many gifts to offer, including their spirituality as a resilient community. Third, the members of on an intercultural church develop the competency of negotiating cultural sameness and difference. Their identity in Christ is also open to diverse cultural articulations of faith, and equips them to reach out to the religious other without compromising their faith in Jesus.

I am convinced that the recent flux of immigrants can open our eyes to a biblical vision of the church that has been in the Bible all along but has also been muddied by the long decades and centuries of the church being "settled"—a fixture in the dominant culture. Furthermore, I have noticed that much scholarly energy has been put into advocacy around issues related to border policy, while less reflection has been done regarding what are we doing as a society and as a church with the migrants and refugees who are already in our midst.

I am writing this book for churches that are anxious about the changes taking place and, therefore, are trying to maintain their cultural identity as much as they can by separating themselves from communities that are different from them. I am writing this book for pastors and church leaders who are in neighborhoods that are segregated or monocultural and who assume that becoming a multicultural or an intercultural church is far away from them.

> The intercultural church is a missional church.

Fear of change and anxiety around maintaining identity are valid concerns, and safe spaces are needed to engage with them. Such feelings should not be dismissed. This book seeks to make safe space for this process of dealing with fears and anxieties about change. It invites churches and leaders to reflect on the profound power of the biblical understanding of the church as a diverse community of sojourners. I hope this book will inspire pastors and church leaders to explore the biblical foundations of what God is calling the church to be in the age of migration. Digging deeper into this biblical vision, even within monocultural settings, can have a transformative power, forming Christians to be better prepared to engage with people who are different from them.

I am writing this book for pastors and leaders of migrant churches who are mourning the loss of the second generation. Many migrant churches end up serving first-generation migrants, and after these people raise their children in the vicinity of the church, they are frustrated that the youth venture out and leave their church to start their own ethnic congregation that worships in the dominant language or to mingle with other congregations that seek to form multicultural or intercultural churches. I am writing this book for pastors and church leaders who are seeking to respond to the ever-growing diversity of the society by reconfiguring themselves as a church—opening its doors, changing its worship, and restructuring its leadership in order to embrace people who come from different racial, ethnic, and linguistic backgrounds.

I hope that this biblical vision of the church will inspire pastors and leaders of both migrant and settled communities, including first-, second-, and third-generation migrants, to take practical steps toward forming intercultural churches where people can worship, fellowship, and serve God and the world together. Our polarized North American society needs the witness of the church. More specifically, the world needs the intercultural church, grounded in the word in order to embody a unity that celebrates a just diversity in the midst of a world that is fractured and divided.

1

What Is an Intercultural Church?

The Bible uses various metaphors to speak about the church.[1] These metaphors include but are not limited to people, family, body, temple, and new creation. Such metaphors do not just function as pictures or images that seek to describe what it means to be a church; they also constitute and shape what the church is about, how it relates to God, and how its members relate to one another and to the world that surrounds them.

One image about the people of God that is used in the Hebrew Bible as well as in the New Testament describes them as sojourners and resident aliens. This image or metaphor is rooted in the reality of the people of Israel in the Hebrew Bible and in the experience of the church in the New Testament. Both groups experienced a life in exile or diaspora and were forced to migrate and live in places that were not their home. Yet not all who were part of the church experienced physical and literal sojourn, and therefore, sojourn and migration function as metaphors pointing to an identity that demands a moral imagination in shaping relationships with God and others who are different. In other words, the identity of the church as a community of sojourners is always experienced literally by some Christians and ascribed metaphorically to other Christians who have settled for a long time. Either way, literal or metaphorical, migration and sojourn bear a promise for those who are anxious and serve as a call to those who are settled to embrace the stranger as oneself.

The Church in the Age of Migration

Recent waves of migration and the change of demographics in North America are calling the church to rediscover the power of seeing itself as a community of migrants and sojourners. It is important, nevertheless, to say at the outset that migration is not a new phenomenon, and varieties of communities have experienced migration in ways that are traumatic and deeply painful. Based on the Doctrine of Discovery, many European nations justified their imperial ambitions by conquering many parts of the Americas, Asia, and Africa, causing the displacement of many indigenous peoples. Colonial and imperial powers enslaved Africans and brought them to the Americas. Civil wars, climate change, religious and political persecutions, and economic distress leave many communities no option other than taking the risk of making the perilous journey of migration. As the church rediscovers its identity as a community of sojourners and migrants, the painful stories of oppression, injustice, and forced migration must be remembered, so that the resilience of those who were forced to migrate continues to inspire the work of justice and so that those who belong to the dominant culture hear the call to use their privilege for the well-being of others.

In the midst of today's political discourse about migration, it is important for the church to think of itself as a community of migrants and sojourners. Xenophobia and stereotyping of migrants dominate campaign rallies; politicians use people's fear of the other and those who are different in order to gain more votes and power. Many policy makers have lost their compassion for the undocumented. Promises to build a wall dash the hopes of those who are dreaming of a better life, deportation separates and divides family members, and the petitions of asylum seekers and refugees are denied—all as a result of politics of fear. Some are attempting to erase the very nature of the United States as a country of immigrants. More striking is the situation of recent migrants with legal status who are trying to fit into the new society yet face racism and tougher policies on migration.

In this environment, the biblical image of the church as a community of migrants becomes even more significant and countercultural. Not only does it call the church to the work of advocacy and solidarity with the refugee, asylum seeker, and migrant, it also calls the church to embody a different way of being in the world—a world that is full of fear, hatred, and walls. As important as it is to talk about borders and welcoming the stranger, it is equally significant to ask: What is the church doing about the migrants who are already here? What kind of society and church are we? What kind of church is God calling us to be in a society that is dominated by politics of assimilation and segregation?

Monocultural, Multicultural, Intercultural

Two metaphors that try to capture how Canadian and American societies deal with cultural differences are the melting pot and the salad bowl. In the melting-pot model, the assumption is that unique cultural identities dissolve to form a new collective identity. In the salad-bowl model, the assumption is that the ingredients keep their distinct character and coexist side by side.

For the most part, congregations and churches function under these models and assumptions. In the monocultural model, the church actively seeks to preserve a particular culture by trying to exclude external influences and by silencing insiders who are seeking change. Thus, difference and change seem to be a threat; relations with outsiders are minimal or nonexistent. In some cases, congregations assume a dominant culture, and while others might be welcomed to join in, they are expected to assimilate into that dominant culture.

The multicultural church celebrates racial, ethnic, theological, and cultural differences. In this model, people stand alongside one another but without influencing or being influenced by one another. Agnes Brazal and Emmanuel De Guzman, in their book *Intercultural Church: Bridge of Solidarity in the Migration Context*, differentiate between multiculturalism and interculturalism in the following way: "Multiculturalism refers to the policy of peaceful co-existence of different cultural communities in one nation-state, with neither intention nor vision of interaction to create a larger community of bonding. Interculturalism not only respects difference but creates a space for the interaction of diverse cultural groups within a society."[2]

So in an intercultural church, the members who come from different cultural, racial, and ethnic backgrounds enter a covenant with one another to worship and fellowship together and serve one another, and to witness to the world about God's reconciling mission in a broken world that longs for peace, justice, and unity. Indeed, for Grace Ji-Sun and Kim Jann Aldredge-Clanton,

> The multicultural church celebrates racial, ethnic, theological, and cultural differences.

Intercultural churches and ministries bring people of various cultures together to learn from one another, giving equal value and power to each culture, preserving cultural differences, and celebrating the variety of cultural traditions. Intercultural churches and ministries are defined by justice, mutuality, respect, equality, understanding, acceptance, freedom, peacemaking, and celebration. In intercultural churches people must be willing to leave the comfort zones of their own separate traditions. . . . They must be willing to embrace difference styles of worship. As people from different cultures interact with one another and build relationships, they grow together and become transformed.[3]

Intercultural Church: A Definition

In light of the recent wave of migration, the church in North America is called by the Spirit to live as a covenantal community that cultivates a decentralizing unity and fosters a just diversity. By a "decentralizing unity," I mean that church members realize there are common beliefs and practices that unify them beyond their specific cultures. And by a "just diversity," I am referring to the equal representation of the different cultural and theological heritages that are present in a given congregation as decision-making and planning for worship and ministries of the church are undertaken. In this covenantal community, differences are received as a gift, not as a threat, and boundaries are not rigid but instead are porous and mutually negotiated. When individuals and groups in the church learn how to claim and be critical of who they are, when they learn how to offer to and to receive from one another, the church embodies an alternative beyond the models of assimilation and segregation. When the church becomes an *intercultural* covenantal community, moving beyond being a *monocultural* or *multicultural* church, it proclaims a message of hope in a polarized and divided world.

Cultural Differences and Boundaries

Underlying the existing models of how the society in North America engages with cultural difference (e.g., melting pot, salad bowl) and the existing models of the church (e.g., the assimilation church, monocultural church, multicultural church) are questions about difference and boundaries. Humans respond differently to difference, whatever that difference is—be it cultural, racial, ethnic, sexual, or economic, or based on gender, ability, age, theology, or being from rural or urban settings. People wonder whether differences are an obstacle or an opportunity. Should people talk about cultural differences? If they do, will this set communities apart from one another? Is it better to focus more on commonalities? Will this bring people closer to one another? Closely related to how communities deal with differences is the question of how these groups of people handle boundaries within the community. Do loose boundaries foster a better community? Do thick boundaries ensure the well-being of the members of the community? Where do communities draw the boundaries? Who draws those boundaries?

These are not new questions. The church at large has thought about them in relation to the ecumenical movement. Local congregations of every generation wrestle with these questions in relation to generational differences and in relation to diverse approaches to theology, worship, and mission. But in this era, these questions are revisited in light of the demographic changes in North American societies due to the flux of migration over the past few decades. The church is called in this era to offer a theological vision in response to racial and ethnic diversity. Does the church perceive difference as a gift from God?

Mitchell R. Hammer, who developed an intercultural development inventory, defines intercultural competence as the ability to understand and adapt behavior to cultural difference and similarity.[4] Individuals are not born interculturally competent; their experiences, education, and willingness to relate to those who are different help them acquire the necessary skills to understand and engage with cultural differences and commonalities. Milton Bennett and Mitchell Hammer speak of a "Developmental Model of Intercultural Sensitivity" or "Intercultural Development Continuum."[5] The continuum reflects the individual's capabilities in dealing with cultural differences and commonalities. The continuum is divided into two mindsets: monocultural and intercultural. Along the continuum are various modes of sensitivity:

> **Does the church perceive difference as a gift from God?**

1. *Denial* is an orientation that likely recognizes more observable cultural differences (e.g., food) but may not notice deeper cultural differences (e.g., conflict resolution styles, expressions of respect, understandings of time or success, etc.) and may avoid or withdraw from cultural differences.

2. *Polarization* is a judgmental orientation that views cultural differences in terms of "us" and "them." Cultural polarization can take the form of defense or reversal. *Defense* is an uncritical view of one's own cultural values and practices and an overly critical view of other cultural values and practices. *Reversal* is an overly critical orientation toward one's own cultural values and practices and an uncritical view of other cultural values and practices.

3. *Minimization* is an orientation that highlights cultural commonality and universal values and principles that

may also mask deeper recognition and appreciation of cultural differences.

4. *Acceptance* is an orientation that recognizes and appreciates patterns of cultural difference and commonality in one's own and other cultures.

5. *Adaptation* is an orientation that is capable of shifting cultural perspective and changing behavior in culturally appropriate and authentic ways.

What this inventory shows is that intercultural competence is a process in which one creates specific and measurable goals in order to move along on the continuum toward adaptation. Another aspect about this inventory that is helpful for intercultural competence is that it invites individuals to claim a cultural location and then look into commonalities with other cultures in order to build bridges of trust and foster a common language. It also empowers individuals to perceive cultural differences as something other than threats or obstacles. Rather, difference is seen as something to be welcomed and celebrated.

Accepting cultural differences is not, however, the end goal. The goal is for individuals to adapt to these cultural differences when they encounter persons who are different from them. While the inventory might be speaking of temporary shifts of cultural perspectives when individuals are embedded in a culture that is different from theirs, I perceive adaptation as a process in which the individuals who come from different cultural backgrounds are willing to be mutually changed and transformed upon knowing and encountering the other. This whole process depends on self-consciousness (self-knowledge) and also openness to know and be known by the other.

The knowledge of self and the other are intertwined with the knowledge of God. John Calvin writes, "Nearly all the wisdom which we possess, that is to say, true and sound wisdom, consists of two parts: the knowledge of God and of ourselves. But, while joined by many bonds, which one precedes and brings forth the other is not easy to discern."[6] To Calvin's thesis about the connection between self-knowledge and the knowledge of God one can add that these two types of knowledge shape and are affected by encountering the other. Henri Nouwen suggests,

> Conversion to God means a simultaneous conversion to the other persons who live with you on this earth. The farmer, the worker, the student, the prisoner, the sick, the black, the white, the weak, the strong, the oppressed and the oppressor, the patient and the one who heals, the tortured and the torturer, the boss and the flunky, not only are they people like you, but they are also called to make themselves heard and to give God a chance to be the God of all.[7]

Knowledge of God and knowledge of self and knowledge of the other are all connected. Because the self and the other are different in many respects and their knowledge of God is diverse and rich, then being in the church with the other yields distinct spiritualties and faith journeys. The members of a church that seeks to become a healthy intercultural church need to learn how to engage with the commonalities and the differences that mark these faith journeys. Developing the skill of negotiating differences and similarities guards the church against falling prey to rejecting cultural diversity in the name of unity, and at the same time, it protects the church against fragmentation in the name of diversity. An intercultural church finds a unity in its worship of the triune God, yet at the same time, this church is formed by the different expressions of faith that emerge from the different cultures that are present within it. The unity of the church does not happen at the expense of its diversity, or as a result of favoring a dominant culture, and the celebration particular of cultural expressions of faith and worship should not be turned into walls that divide the church.

For some, this vision of an intercultural church might seem too perfect to be actualized or too much of an ideal, requiring so much work that it might not, therefore, be suitable for the church here and now. It is important to remember that such a vision for the church is grounded in Pentecost, when the Spirit was reaching out to the diaspora communities with the good news of Jesus Christ, and it is inspired by the visions of worship offered to God by people from different languages, tribes, peoples, and ethnicities in Revise to "Revelation 4–7." This is not just a memory of the past or a dream about the future, but rather it is a manifestation of a realized eschatology in which God has entered the world to form a worshipping community

> This vision of an intercultural church might seem too perfect to be actualized.

that is diverse. The fact that the church has failed to live up to this mission of God should not hinder the church from listening to the call of the Spirit to be transformed, even if this happens gradually and one step at a time.

Acts 10 as a Model for the Intercultural Church

The transformation of a given congregation from being monocultural or multicultural is not an easy process, and it is hard work that can endure and persevere if there is a vision for it. The story of Peter and Cornelius offers a vision of the movement of the Spirit of God to push the church beyond its walls and to encounter God's mission in the world. It is intriguing to note that the transformation happened when there were visions: Peter and Cornelius saw visions, and thus they were both moved by God to reach out to the other who was quite different.

The story as recorded in Acts 10 provides a framework for thinking about the vision of an intercultural church. This framework begins with a clear statement that the church is God's project and so does not belong to a specific culture or group of people. Although the church embraces all people from whatever cultures, after all it is God's mission and not the mission of a particular culture. Furthermore, this story highlights the fact that for an intercultural church to come into being, the communities that come from different backgrounds need to be open to being converted and transformed. In this church, the need is mutual, fellowship is necessary, and healthy boundaries maintain the well-being of the body.

The Church Is God's Project

On the surface, the text of Acts 10 sets up readers to see the drastic differences between Peter and Cornelius. These differences would render a communion between the two impossible. Cornelius is a Roman citizen. As an officer in the Roman army, he is a man of authority. He is part of the imperial system. In contrast, Peter is a marginalized and powerless Jew, a follower of Jesus Christ; he lives in the house of another, Simon. The text points out ethnic, religious, economic, and political differences. Indeed, when Peter encounters Cornelius, he says, "You yourselves know that it is unlawful for a Jew to associate with or visit a Gentile" (10:28), yet the story ends with the narrator's report that "they [Cornelius's family and friends] invited him to stay for several days" (10:48). How did this development take place? What power or agent was at play in deconstructing the walls of difference that separated Cornelius and Peter while creating a space and a time for fellowship the set the church onto a new path, the path toward becoming an intercultural community?

The story in Acts 10 lays down a foundational theological claim that functions as the cornerstone of an intercultural church. As the narrative unfolds, the triune God appears as the key player in breaking the boundaries between Jews and gentiles, forming a renewed faith community. That the church is God's project is apparent in three ways in the narrative: (1) God, not the church, takes the initiative. (2) Peter's sermon (10:34–43) emphasizes the lordship of Christ, and (3) the Spirit manifests its freedom as it is poured out on the gentiles (10:44–45). God orchestrates the scene for Peter, the Jew, and Cornelius, the gentile, to meet. It was God who accepted the prayers of Cornelius. God sent an angel and gave visions to Peter and Cornelius. When a religious tradition seemed to hinder the movement of God's reconciling mission in the world, it was God who made it clear to Peter in the vision that "what God has made clean, you must not call profane" (10:15). After Peter arrives in Caesarea, he announces that although it is unlawful for him as a Jew to associate with gentiles, "God has shown me that I should not call anyone profane or unclean" (10:28). In other words, the mission belongs to God, and it is God who sets and breaks the boundaries.

When Peter preached to Cornelius and his household, the sermon focused on the lordship of Jesus Christ: "he is Lord of all" (10:36). In his life and ministry, empowered by the Holy Spirit, Jesus Christ proclaimed a message of peace and liberty from the principalities and powers: "he went about doing good and healing all who were oppressed by the devil" (10:38). Through his death and resurrection, he offers forgiveness of sin to those who believe in him, and he "is the one ordained by God as judge of the living and the dead" (10:42). That Jesus is seen as the Lord of all shows that power belongs to God, and all peoples from different tribes, ethnic groups, and nations are equal in receiving this message of peace that God proclaimed through Jesus. The nature of the lordship of Jesus is that of peace, freedom, and healing. Because Jesus is judge and lord, all who abuse their power to marginalize and oppress other human beings are called to repent, and all who feel alienated and disempowered are called to trust in Jesus, who sets them free and heals them from the wounds of oppression and rejection.

The Spirit of God is also active in the story. While Peter was baffled by the vision that he had seen, the Spirit informed him about the messengers that Cornelius had sent, and the Spirit commanded Peter to go with them without hesitation (10:19–20). One of the fascinating ironies of the story can be seen in the way the Spirit came upon the gentiles who gathered in the house of Cornelius. While Peter was trying to explain God's acceptance of the gentiles, and as he went on to summarize the liberating and healing message of the gospel, the Spirit fell upon all of those who were gathered: "While Peter was still speaking, the Holy Spirit fell upon all who heard the word" (10:44). The pouring out of the Spirit on the gentiles recalls the powerful presence of the Spirit at Pentecost. This is evident in the verbal connections between both episodes, which include being astonished (2:7, 12 / 10:45), speaking in tongues (2:11 / 10:46), exalting God (2:11 / 10:46), and the gift of the Holy Spirit (2:38 / 10:45).[8] What is interesting here is that there was no chance for the gentiles to proclaim anything; they did not have their "come to the pulpit" moment. Instead, the Spirit acted freely beyond human plans. The freedom of the Spirit left the circumcised believers astonished (10:45–46; cf. 2:7).

It is evident in this narrative that it is the triune God who holds the authority in the midst of the church and that the triune God is the agent that effects a change in the church by breaking down the boundaries that separate believers who come from different ethnic backgrounds to form an intercultural worshipping community. Healthy relationships between believers in the church—that is, for the purpose of this discussion, relationships that embrace cultural differences—will flourish when the sovereign God, the risen Lord, and the free Spirit take their rightful central place in the life of the church. Living up to God's vision of a church in which people of different cultures can worship, fellowship, and serve together is difficult when members of the church want the church to revolve around them and their particular values, habits, needs, worldviews, theologies, worship styles, and practices while ignoring the contribution that others can offer to enrich the life of faith.

Relationships may be distorted by ideologies of oppression and marginalization, causing church members to walk into their relationships in and outside of the church asking certain questions: Who is at the center? Whose terms and conditions will the relationship follow and adhere to? Who has the authority? These questions are very significant for the well-being of the faith community, especially because people do not enter these relationships on equal footing. There is a long history of privilege and power and a long history of oppression and marginalization. I am proposing, though, that the church should take these questions seriously but without losing the theological perspective that when God is God, those who possess power will use it for the well-being of the other, and those who are marginalized will experience liberation and justice. The statement that God is at the center of the beliefs and practices of the church is not a theological rug under which sins of injustices and alienation are swept. To say that God is at the center is to make a theological claim that keeps those who lust after power in check and liberates those who experience estrangement and oppression, so that all peoples who come from different cultures can experience justice, love, and belonging.

When God occupies the place at the center of the church and when there is trust in God as God exercises God's authority, humans learn what it means to be a human being. Cornelius, the army officer, gives up his authority when he bows down to Peter (Acts 10:25). Peter urges him to stand up, saying, in effect, "Why are you bowing to me? I am a human like you." In saying, "I am a human like you," Peter asserts his humanness as well as the humanness of Cornelius. Cornelius is a human being, and now Peter realizes that he cannot speak of other human beings as "profane or unclean" (10:28). That is, when Peter recognizes that God is the one who holds the authority, he also realizes that he cannot see other human beings according to his own categories, but he now sees other human beings based on how God sees them.

There may be no reason to be suspicious of highlighting the sovereignty of God as a central theological claim, because of fear that such a claim would perpetuate the supremacy of those who think God is on their side. Abuse of such a theological claim has happened before in the history of Christianity. Yet this narrative shows another possibility for restoring the belief in divine authority—namely, that humans recognize each other as equal children of God. In contrast to colonialism, sexism, racism, and homophobia, which dehumanize others, affirming the centrality of God enables humans to see the dignity of the other because God is not partial toward anyone. Peter highlights this quality about God as his starting point in his sermon to Cornelius: "I truly understand that God shows no partiality" (10:34). The

God who does not show partiality called and commanded Peter and Cornelius to reach out to each other. Because they recognize who they are in relation to God, they show submission and obedience to what God commanded them to do. Although Peter and Cornelius were afraid and baffled because of the visions they saw, both of them show a great deal of submission and obedience to God's instructions. Their trust in God leads each of them to trust human beings who are different from them to fulfill their needs and answer their questions.

The Need Is Mutual

One thing that is very clear in the story is that these two human beings, Peter and Cornelius, need one another. God could have simply told Cornelius what he needed to do. The Spirit could have simply come down upon Cornelius without the trouble of sending to Peter and waiting a few days for his arrival. But God had planned for a meeting to take place between Cornelius and Peter. Cornelius's knowledge about what God is up to is partial. Therefore, he sends for Peter, and he needs Peter to tell him what to do. When Peter finally had come to his house, Cornelius eagerly announces, "So now all of us are here in the presence of God to listen to all that the Lord has commanded you to say" (10:33). Four days of anticipation had passed since Peter and Cornelius had their visions. While Cornelius is waiting for Peter to reveal to him what he is supposed to do, Peter also seeks to piece together the puzzle of his vision, whose meaning apparently hinges on encountering an outsider (10:13, 17, 29).

Finally, Peter is at the house of Cornelius in a territory where he should not be, and after crossing ethnic and religious boundaries, he seeks an explanation, saying, "Now may I ask why you sent for me?" (10:29). Peter is still hungry, not for food, but for his eyes to be opened so that he can see what God is up to in bringing him to this risky, dangerous encounter with a gentile. Peter already expressed a recognition that the vision of food that he saw was not necessarily about actual food but rather about people, and the change of view is not only about dietary law but also about crossing boundaries through relationships. Peter and Cornelius are looking for meaning, and the meaning lies in their encounter with the other. Both have something to offer, but both need the piece of the puzzle that the other person has. God's mission in the world happens at its best when people cross boundaries to encounter others who are different from them. We human beings will always possess a partial understanding of God and God's work, but we can grasp a fuller understanding if we recognize the partiality of our knowledge and if we seek to see the truth with the other who is different from us.

In a plain sense, hunger for food refers to a natural human need to survive. Yet in this narrative, hunger and eating refer to building new relationships of crossing religious and ethnic boundaries. While Peter's hosts (Simon the tanner and his family) were preparing a meal for Peter, who was famished, God was preparing another kind of meal for him: "He became hungry and wanted something to eat; and while it was being prepared, he fell into a trance" (10:10). In other words, while Peter's physical hunger could have been satisfied by the simple meal that his hosts were preparing, God was at work meeting his need with a meal he did not expect. God was stirring Peter's appetite for something new. Peter was not going to have the usual meal that would satisfy his physical hunger.

Being in the church is a way of expressing one's hunger for fellowship, a hunger that could be filled with having the same meal every time. But what this narrative is pointing to is that God prepares new meals for those who spend time in prayer to discern what God is calling them to do. Being in such a state of hunger and at the same time anticipating a new type of meal can make people vulnerable, because they do not know what to expect. It takes courage to expose one's vulnerability and need for the other. Some are more comfortable giving, while others are constantly receiving. While some think they have nothing to offer, others assume they have the solution to every need. Healthy relationships depend on mutuality in giving and receiving. It is important to recognize the impact of socioeconomic privilege or disenfranchisement on how individuals see themselves as subjects capable of giving and receiving in a set of relationships. Preparing individuals emotionally and mentally with regard to cultural understandings of giving and receiving is a significant factor in the success of cross-cultural relationships. Self-awareness is the key to negotiating this process of expressing one's needs and opening oneself to the other to receive the gifts that are offered. Self-awareness also enables individuals to name what they can offer without feeling abused or taken advantage of.

It takes a vision to realize one's deep needs for the other who is different, and it takes divine support and courage for one to risk exposing one's needs for the other. It does not matter *what* people give or receive, but it matters *that* they give and receive, because it is this very posture of mutual need and mutual hospitality that prevents relationships in the church from becoming coercive or manipulative. It is this openness that creates room for the Spirit of God to transform the community into an intercultural church. Since members of the church are people who are in need of one another and who have something to offer to each other, the church will continue to experience change, and the identities of its members will be fluid and not rigid.

> It takes a vision to realize one's deep needs for the other who is different.

Conversion Is Mutual

The story of Peter and Cornelius is a story of mutual conversion, and it is an ongoing process. Both parties were transformed through the work of God in response to the Holy Spirit and through the encounter with the other. Anthony Robinson and Robert Wall provide an apt description of the kind of conversion that is needed:

> Conversion is often understood as conversion from no faith to faith, or from one faith to another. Furthermore, conversion is just as often understood to be something

that happens just once in a person's life. Peter's experience throws a monkey wrench into those assumptions: as a follower of Jesus, he is converted to a new understanding of the church's faith and mission, one that leads him to step across boundaries and barriers that had, up to this point, seemed impenetrable. Not only as a believer and follower of Christ, but also as an apostle and leader of the church, Peter finds his mind opened and his life redirected. Conversion continues.[9]

Both Cornelius and Peter saw visions. That is, both needed to see the world in a new way. Seeing the world in a new way meant understanding better God's activity in their lives and in the lives of others. Thus, it is best to think of this story not as a story of conversion of gentiles but as a story of conversion of both the church and the gentiles. While Cornelius needed a single vision, Peter needed the content of the vision to be repeated three times. It takes insiders three times what it takes outsiders to resolve to respond to God's work in the world. It takes much prayer and effort to convert insiders, because insiders often think they know God's ways too well to grasp that God can do something outside of those patterns.

Conversion in the case of Cornelius meant taking his piety a further step. He recognizes that God accepts his longing for God, that God is seeking to be in communion with him as God has given him the gift of the Spirit, and that Cornelius is to be part of the emerging faith community that is the church. Cornelius the Roman officer has to think about his power in a new way.

Cornelius is a commander of one hundred soldiers (cf. Luke 7:1–10; 23:47). Although he represents the imperial power of Rome, he does not let this power stand between him and God. Cornelius bows down to Peter, expressing his eagerness to learn from Peter what God wants to reveal to him. Cornelius's conversion is made possible by an encounter with Peter, the Jew. Cornelius's piety is directed both toward fearing God (offering prayers) and toward other humans (giving alms). Cornelius's conversion is better understood in terms of seeing what he was doing as something that was in an alignment with the good news of Jesus, yet he needed to see the relationship with God not only as a human effort of seeking God but essentially as a divine initiative. The divine initiative is clear in that Cornelius and those who were with him did not need to confess their sins or repent or change their ways in order to receive the gift of the Spirit. Indeed, the text notes that the Spirit fell upon all who heard the word while Peter was speaking. The gift of the Spirit, which is the ultimate sign of communion with God, prepares the way for communion and fellowship with the circumcised believers.

Cornelius and his household then get to be baptized to become members of the covenantal community, the church, which is made up of both Jews and gentiles. In this covenantal community, the Spirit brings together people who are different from one another in order to glorify God, and Jesus as Lord (10:36, 46). But for this mission of the church to happen, the Spirit is at work converting not only those who might be deemed outsiders but also those who might consider themselves insiders. Eric Barreto explains that Acts 10 is a story of the conversion of both Cornelius and Peter: "We should also notice that this is not a simple story of Cornelius's conversion. Yes, his encounter with the Holy Spirit must have transformed him, but perhaps it is Peter and his companions who leave this scene most changed. Proclamation on the move among strangers will not change only them; it will change us, too, for God has already moved ahead of us to be in their midst."[10]

Peter's conversion is about recognizing God's work beyond what Peter has taken for granted as normal and familiar. Through the visions and through the encounter with the other (Cornelius), Peter comes to the realization that God is not bound to a set of traditions, but rather God is free to act in the way that God sees fit to accomplish God's reconciling mission in the world. That is, there is a conversion toward who God is and who Peter is as a human being. Yet the conversion is not just about a personal relationship with God. It is also about a way of relating to the other. It is about being transformed to be in community with others. Joel Green defines conversion in Luke-Acts in the following way:

> Converts are those who, enabled by God, have undergone a redirectional shift and now persist along the Way with the community of those faithfully serving God's eschatological purposes as this is evident in the life, death, and exaltation of the Lord Jesus Christ, and whose lives are continually being formed through the Spirit at work in and through practices constitutive of this community.[11]

As a convert, Peter is enabled by God through visions and through the work of the Spirit; his conversion also happens as the boundaries of the community are reshaped. Peter's conversion is about a paradigm shift, not only in his understanding of who God is and of who Peter is as a human being, but also of who the other is. At the beginning of the vision, he says to God, "By no means, Lord; for I have never eaten anything that is profane or unclean" (Acts 10:14). To which God responds, "What God has made clean, you must not call profane" (10:15). Not only does this happen three times, but Peter is able to understand this vision only when he encounters the other, when he goes to Cornelius. Peter says to Cornelius, "You yourselves know that it is unlawful for a Jew to associate with or to visit a Gentile; but God has shown me that I should not call anyone profane or unclean" (10:28). The vision is about a paradigm shift in the way Peter and the church think about God's work in the church and beyond.

Unclean and *impure* are terms used in the Old Testament to speak of how fit the people are to worship God, to approach the holy, and to participate in rituals. Eating particular animals would have made people unfit to worship; some bodily discharges would turn a human being into a contaminating, impure entity that other people should avoid in order to maintain their cleanness. Mary Douglas suggests a rationale for understanding the categories of clean/unclean, including why it is permitted to eat some animals and not others because some are considered impure. According to Douglas, these impure or unclean things transgress given boundaries.[12] They do not fit in a particular category. An ostrich, even though it is a bird, is considered unclean because it does not fly, so it does not fit well in its category.

This approach for explaining the notions of clean/unclean does not explain all the dietary laws that we find in Leviticus 11, yet it has proven helpful in understanding some aspects of the structural framework of the priestly traditions.[13] These categories of clean and unclean were extended to speak about the relation between the Israelites and the non-Israelites. Leviticus 20:24–25, for example, reads,

> I am the Lord your God; I have separated you from the peoples. You shall therefore make a distinction between the clean animal and the unclean, and between the unclean bird and the clean; you shall not bring abomination on yourselves by animal or by bird or by anything with which the ground teems, which I have set apart for you to hold unclean.

A similar connection between eating habits and relationships between Jews and gentiles persisted in the Second Temple period. According to some first-century Jewish traditions, gentiles were regarded as unclean. Their eating habits and their sexual behaviors made them unclean, so they were seen as an other.[14] According to a strict religious view, a relation between a Jew and a gentile would be framed by categories of clean and unclean. Maintaining the boundary between the clean and the unclean was vital to the well-being of the people and to the stability of their religious identity. Through the visions and through encountering the work of the Spirit in others, Peter was converted into

God's liberating work that reconfigures the boundaries of the community to show inclusion and hospitality.

It is important to note that though the conversions of Peter and Cornelius are dramatic, they are not sudden. For the transformation to happen, both men needed to take some prior steps. Peter was staying with a tanner, who would have been regarded as an unclean, because tanners are in contact with dead animals. It is possible to see Peter's stay with a tanner as a step forward in Peter's journey toward understanding how God is about to change the paradigm of Jewish-gentile relations.[15] Cornelius's piety and his new understanding of God's revelation also prepared him to become a member of God's community, since his charity sought the well-being of others around him. For conversion to happen for both Cornelius and Peter, two other conditions are in place: both of them received divine visions while they were praying. In the case of Cornelius, it is stated implicitly: the third hour of the afternoon (the ninth hour of the day) was an hour of prayer (10:3; cf. 3:1). Peter's praying is expressed explicitly in the text (10:9). Not only do both men pray, but both of them are obedient to the divine word, even though it is not clear where it will lead them. Their obedience underlines their trust in God.

In the contemporary context of the church, people are not classified according to the categories of clean and unclean. Yet people in society and the church use a similar logic. People categorize and classify others based on their own terms, worldviews, definitions, and what they consider normal. Thus, churches and communities are often defined based on categories of ethnicity, color, race, gender, sexuality, economic and social status, dietary preferences, ethical decisions, abilities, and so on. Relationships and lack of relationships within a community and with other communities are influenced and shaped by cultural and religious worldviews that determine who is in and who is out of the circles of a community or church. It is clear that in Acts 10, the Holy Spirit calls the church members to examine how their worldviews may affect the ways they relate to other members of the body. For an intercultural church to be formed in a healthy way, the Holy Spirit calls the members of the church to mutual conversion. The change should not fall on the shoulders of one group of people within the church in order to make them fit a presupposed way of being a church. Mutual conversion means that the members of the church recognize that they and their culture are not the center of the church and that, for an intercultural church to be born, there has to be a change in how the church is defined and done in terms of its mission, worship, and fellowship.

Different groups contribute to the life of the church based on what is distinctive about their culture, but they should also be open to adapting to the other groups with whom they seek to be a church. When each group adjusts and adapts, that means something will change about each group, and together they will give birth to something new. In this new configuration of the church, people negotiate what to maintain about their distinctive cultural identities, but they also adopt a posture of flexibility and openness to change in order to welcome others into their lives. Mutual conversion relies on attentiveness to the way the Holy Spirit redraws the boundaries between the members of the church.

Building an intercultural church depends on the recognition that people's theological worldviews are not a finished project and that the way the Spirit calls the church to become intercultural is an ongoing process that unfolds as the church members reflect on their practices of worship, fellowship, and ministry. That is, there is not one standard model for the church to be intercultural that should be applied in the same way everywhere. Rather, what unfolds is a process of conversion in which each congregation listens to what the Spirit is calling them to be and do as an intercultural covenantal church in a given space and time with specific challenges and gifts that the Spirit provides to deal with these challenges. Yet the church has to start somewhere; it starts, and then it modifies its practices of worship, ministry, and fellowship.

> There is not one standard model for the church to be intercultural that should be applied in the same way everywhere.

Fellowship Is Necessary

The story of the conversion of Peter and Cornelius ends with a request from the gentile believers for Peter and the circumcised believers to remain with them for a time. Fellowship is a central aspect of the identity of the church in the book of Acts: "They devoted themselves to the apostles' teaching and fellowship, to the breaking of bread and the prayers" (Acts 2:42). Those who believed were together much of the time, and all that they had was shared among them (2:44–46). As they shared time and possessions, one of the rituals that sustained and deepened their sense of fellowship was eating together: "they broke bread at home and ate their food with glad and generous hearts" (2:46). Sharing meals together and providing for the needs of all brought much joy and gladness to the members of the church. Sharing meals is a significant aspect of covenant theology in the Old and the New Testaments. Isaac and Abimelech ate together as part of their peace treaty (Genesis 26); Moses and the seventy elders ate before God following the establishment of the covenant (Exodos 24); Jesus ate and drank with his disciples when he established the new covenant (Luke 22).

Sharing meals could provide valuable opportunities for deep encounters among people who come from different cultural backgrounds and seek to build an intercultural society or a church. Here, I am not referring to eating diverse cuisines by going to restaurants or by getting recipes on the internet, although these are good steps toward expanding one's appetite for cultural difference. Rather, I am referring to spending time with others who are culturally different, cooking together, and eating together. Food is an essential aspect of cultural identity and a tasty way of building deep intercultural relationships. When it comes to food, there are traditional meals and newly invented meals; there are ethnic meals that have different flavors and aroma; there are homemade meals and fast-food meals. Food offers ways for a community to grow in its intercultural competencies. Food also helps as a medium through which communities learn how to share with others their cultural heritage and ways to receive others and their cuisine as a gift that expands one's palate for otherness. Food is a need, but it is also a desire. It has obligatory aspects but also optional characteristics. People might push themselves to try new kinds of meals, but they will likely refrain from foods they are allergic to. Food could also function as a medium for negotiating boundaries: some people are allergic to specific products, while others have dietary preferences (vegetarian, vegan, and so on). Food helps communities navigate their intercultural relations in the church. In the Peter-Cornelius narrative, food was the medium through which God revealed to Peter God's vision for integrating the gentiles in God's people; thus, it was through food that God called Peter into new relationships, and it was through food that Peter and Cornelius showed hospitality to the stranger (10:23, 48).

Healthy Boundaries Are Necessary

Forming an intercultural church is not about the loss of identity, and fellowship does not mean loss of boundaries. The final verses of Acts 10 point to another direction in which fellowship is possible and boundaries are crossed without the loss of what is unique or particular about the individuals involved in these intercultural relationships. Acts 10:45 refers to Peter and those who had come with him from Joppa as "the circumcised believers," and the same verse reports the pouring of the Spirit on Cornelius and his family, saying, "the gift of the Holy Spirit had been poured out even on the Gentiles." Both groups maintain what is distinctive about them. But what is unique about each group, which initially would have rendered this relationship impossible, no longer stands in the way of deep encounter and profound relationship. The work of the Spirit helped these two communities maintain who they are, but at the same time the Spirit empowered them not to stumble over their differences. In an intercultural church, cultural identities do not dissolve or assimilate into a dominant culture, nor do they stand as obstacles on the way to genuine communion. Cultural identities become the means through which different communities express themselves and by which the members of the church get to know God in new ways as they learn to understand that they are in relation to the other and not over against the other. In an intercultural church, the members do not get fixated on their own identities, but pay attention to the new thing that the Spirit is creating when people bearing these identities worship together, fellowship together, and serve together.

The unity that the Spirit fosters in the church is not based on power or control. Sometimes it is easy to confuse unity with hegemony (control or dominant power) and justice with diversity. Unity allows for diversity, while hegemony stifles justice. The health of the church as a covenantal community depends on fostering a unity that flourishes by embracing a just diversity. By that, I mean diversity that cultivates equality and shares power in order to build a healthy church. Such a vision of the church is grounded in the

> The unity that the Spirit fosters in the church is not based on power or control.

politics of the Spirit, who equips all believers with the gifts necessary for the life and mission of the church.

To experience the unity of the church in the Spirit and to maintain a just diversity and to foster genuine transformative relationships, the different cultural communities that are involved in the church must be transparent about how they think culturally about boundaries. An intercultural covenantal church can emerge when the communities involved mutually establish appropriate boundaries. Integration in the church should not happen through the loss of boundaries but rather through a negotiation in which the different parties are seen as equal. Negotiating the boundaries entails learning when to cross the boundaries and when to maintain them. It is not about existing in segregated communities, but it is not about eliminating all boundaries either. It is about reaching a mutual decision on when and how to cross the boundaries. These negotiations are significant for building a church that values unity, because in unity, individuals realize that there is a reality about the church that transcends their specific cultures. That transcendent reality of the church lies in the fact that it is meant to be intercultural and covenantal. Although the church is more than any particular cultural expression, it will always be made of and conditioned by the historical reality of the identities of its members.

Discussion Questions

1. How often do you think of your church or faith community as a group of sojourners or aliens? Why?

2. Notice the metaphors of culture (melting pot and salad bowl) described on p. 14. What is the main characteristic of each? Which best describes your view of society? Of your church?

3. How are the terms *multiculturalism* and *interculturalism* compared and contrasted? (See especially pp. 14–16.) Why does the author encourage churches and faith communities to be intercultural?

4. Commonly, people in a church or faith community have differing ways of understanding intercultural sensitivities. Review the modes of sensitivity listed on p. 18–19. Which mode seems to capture your individual sensitivity best? Why? Which mode do you think best captures the sensitivity of your church or faith community? Why?

5. In what important ways does the story of Peter and Cornelius in Acts 10 lift up the themes of interculturalism? What can be learned from the story?

6. What is one new idea or concept you learned in this chapter? Why is it important?

7. Which of the following statements best describes your church or faith community? Discuss your responses.
   a. We are fully intercultural.
   b. We are not at all intercultural.
   c. We need to move toward becoming intercultural.
   d. We have a confused sense of who we are.
   e. Becoming intercultural would be a big challenge for us.

2

Strangers Ourselves: Reading the Bible as Sojourners

What difference does it make for the readers of the Scriptures to claim their identity as sojourners? Many readers of the Bible know very well how to read the Bible through the lens of the sojourner because they themselves have chosen to migrate or been forced to migrate from their home country to another country to start a new life. For individuals or communities claiming the identity of sojourner, this experience is deeply embedded in their cultural memory. As recent migrants read the Bible, it can evoke their painful experience of the world, feelings of estrangement, loss, and disorientation. Their reading of the Bible is concurrently shaped by their hopes, resilience, and ability to see life through multiple cultural lenses.

However, there are many other readers of the Bible whose ancestors migrated a long time ago and have been settled for decades or centuries in a country. As a result, these communities read the Bible through their experience as a settled community. The communities that read the Bible through their experience of settlement quite often bring to the text a sense of continuity in relation to land and place and a sense of familiarity with and orientation toward the surrounding cultures. Such readers of the Bible may have lost contact with the feelings that the alien experiences, so their response to issues of migration and the integration of newcomers is marked by hesitancy and fear at best and racism and xenophobia in worst cases. Their reading of the Bible glosses over the fact that most of the Bible was written by communities of faith (the Israelites and the early church) whose communal experience of the world was quite often marked by exodus, exile, sojourn, and diaspora. Whether readers of the Bible are recent migrants or belong to a settled community, they must engage with the biblical story through the lens of the people of Israel or the church and must wrestle with the fact that these communities spoke of their relationship with God from the sociopolitical and cultural location of exiles and sojourners.

Reading the Bible through the eyes of migrants can be disorienting and destabilizing to communities that have been settled for a long time. This process of reading can create a space for recent migrants to express their anxieties and hopes. Reading through the eyes of migrants calls the settled readers to remember that being sojourners is part of who they are, and such a memory is capable of producing empathy toward those who are experiencing physical and literal displacement and estrangement. Empathy, which is grounded in real experiences and in the collective memory of a community's history, calls these communities to welcome those strangers, do justice, and integrate the alien other. These same texts that address the communities that have settled for a long time also address the readers of the Bible who have chosen to migrate or were forced to migrate. As these communities experience anxieties, fear of rejection, injustice, and the trauma of alienation, the Bible recenters them and reorients them, giving

> Reading the Bible through the eyes of migrants can be disorienting and destabilizing.

them hope as recipients of divine promises that deepen in them a sense of belonging and rootedness. As a result, these sojourning communities can become bold in claiming the gifts that God blesses them with and can be courageous in sharing these blessings with the community in whose midst they dwell.

Sojourn and Promise: Ancestral Narratives in Genesis

If a group of church members were asked to name a recurring theme in the stories of the ancestors of Israel, the answer would likely be "the promise." From the beginning of God's call to Abraham to move, God promised him a nation, a blessing, and a land to possess (Gen 12:1–3). These promises were renewed over and over in the narrative of Genesis because they were constantly questioned and threatened. Barrenness made the fulfillment of the promise of progeny complicated (Genesis 16; 21; 25), and various famines (Genesis 12; 26; 42–50) and the nomadic lifestyle required moving all the time. Although the promise is a central aspect of the stories of the ancestors, there is another, forgotten aspect of their identity. To understand their stories fully, we need to recognize that they were sojourners and resident aliens.

Abraham identifies himself in exactly this way when he says, "I am a stranger and an alien residing among you; give me property among you for a burying place, so that I may bury my dead out of my sight" (Gen 23:4). God appears to Isaac and commands him to reside as an alien: "Reside in this land as an *alien*, and I will be with you, and will bless you" (Gen 26:3). When Jacob goes down to Egypt, Pharaoh asks him, "How many are the years of your life?" and Jacob replies, "The years of my earthly *sojourn* are one hundred thirty; few and hard have been the years of my life. They do not compare with the years of the life of my ancestors during their long sojourn" (Gen 47:8–9). This identity is declared to the whole people of Israel in the midst of the Jubilee laws. God addresses the whole people, saying, "The land shall not be sold in perpetuity, for the land is mine; with me you are but aliens and tenants" (Lev 25:23). In the New Testament, Peter addresses the churches that are in the diaspora, saying, "Beloved, I urge you as aliens and exiles to abstain from the desires of the flesh that wage war against the soul" (1 Peter 2:11).

Bearing in mind this description of the ancestors—Israel and the church as sojourners and migrants—I suggest that readers of the Bible who identify with the ancestors or read through the lens of the Israelites and the church must reflect on what this status of being migrants demands of them as they respond to contemporary movements of migration. I believe that reading the stories of the ancestors with migration in mind calls us to remember how the ancestors' well-being depended on the generosity of those whom we might think of as outsiders (the Hittites in the case of Abraham, the Philistines in the case of Isaac, and the Egyptians in the case of Jacob). As I will show in this chapter, the memory of the people of Israel being sojourners in Egypt is constantly brought to the fore as an ethical motivation for the people to do justice to the resident alien in their midst. Furthermore, the story of Joseph underlines an important aspect about the relationship between migrant and host communities—namely, mutual need and mutual contribution. Remembering one's story of migration, recognizing one's dependence on and need of the other, offering one's gifts to the other, and doing justice for the marginalized prepare the members of the church to work toward becoming an intercultural church.

Abraham and the Hittites

Living as sojourners and migrants underlines an important aspect regarding human existence: the need to rely on the promises of God and the generosity of others. When Sarah dies, Abraham, who received the promise of the land from God on various occasions, is looking for a place to bury his wife. During those hard times of loss and grief, Abraham's ability to fulfill his duty to his deceased wife—that is, to honor her by burying her—depends on his relationship with his neighbors, the Hittites. While the text of Genesis 23:7 describes the Hittites as "the people of the land," Abraham identifies himself by saying, "I am a stranger and an alien residing among you; give me property among you for a burying place, so that I may bury my dead out of my sight" (Gen 23:4). Here Abraham describes himself as a "migrant" (*ger*) and as a "resident alien" (*toshav*). These two words form "a more or less fixed phrase: he is a settler come from foreign parts."[1]

Although the land was promised to Abraham and his descendants, he does not use force to acquire the land; instead, he insists on buying it from its owners. It is possible that Abraham's peaceful attitude toward both the land and the other inhabitants of the land was formed by his understanding of his identity as a stranger and a resident alien. The attitude of the Hittites is equally inspiring, for they offer Abraham the cave and the field for free so that he can bury his wife. Although Abraham ends up buying the field from the Hittites, the text shows that the Hittites were concerned above all about Abraham's need to honor his wife and to have a sense of closure; they repeatedly say to him, "Bury your dead" (23:11, 15). It is also interesting to note that Abraham, Isaac, Rebecca, and Leah are later buried in that same burial site, and it is there that Jacob asks his children to bury him at the end of his sojourn in Egypt.

This episode highlights how the identity of being a sojourner in the land informs the ancestors' relation to the land and to their neighbors in the land: this relationship is marked by peace and mutual respect and dignity. But the episode also shows how, at times of loss and grief, a migrant can find comfort and support in good relationships with neighbors. The well-being of those whom we see as insiders relies on the hospitality and generosity of those whom we might see as outsiders. What change does it make if the ones who were offered promises by God are the contemporary migrants and if the Hittites are the readers of the Bible who have settled for generations? It is equally important for readers of the Bible to read the story from the perspective of the sojourning ancestors who live by the promise and to read also from the perspective of the Hittites in this narrative. In this latter case, the readers need to ask themselves about the respect and hospitality that the text calls them to offer to the migrant or sojourner in their midst.

Isaac and the Philistines

The dual identity of sojourner living by the promise and settler living like a migrant also informs the relationship between Isaac and the Philistines found in Genesis 26. Because of a famine, Isaac has to move from the Negeb to settle among the Philistines, where his life, survival, and well-being depend on the generosity and hospitality of the outsiders. After Isaac has already moved to be with Abimelech, king of the Philistines, God appears to him and commands him to reside as an alien: "Reside in this land as an alien, and I will be with you, and will bless you" (Gen 26:4). God's imperative to Isaac to dwell in the land as a sojourner is unique in that it is the only time in the ancestral narratives that "sojourning" is divinely commanded. Not only does the well-being of the ancestor of Israel depend on the other inhabitants of the land, but we also notice that God commands Isaac to claim his identity as a sojourner, as a stranger. Elisabeth Kennedy writes, "Sojourn for Isaac, then, is not simply a given reality that expresses the fact of his foreign origins relative to the territory promised. It is rather a behavioral mandate."[2]

Being a sojourner heightens the anxieties surrounding being unwelcome or rejected. Migrants experience vulnerability and disorientation as they leave behind all that is familiar and embark on a journey into the unknown. Therefore, the command to sojourn is followed by divine promises are offered to Isaac (Gen 26:3–5). These promises meant to empower him and give him a sense of orientation as a foreigner in a new residence. These promises include a divine blessing, an accompaniment, and a sense of connection with the land and the ancestors.

> Migrants experience vulnerability and disorientation as they leave behind all that is familiar and embark on a journey into the unknown.

Migrants who are forced to move for economic reasons seek a better quality of life for themselves and for their children. When people migrate, they may feel lonely, and they long for a community that welcomes them and integrates them. Migrants also struggle with the feeling of uprootedness—that is, they suffer from the loss of being connected to a homeland or a community, and they feel as if they do not fully belong or fit into their new home. Therefore, God addresses those fears by offering Isaac promises that connect him with his ancestors, deepen his roots in the land, offer him a blessing, and assure him of divine companionship: "I am with you" (Gen 26:24).

When readers of the Bible read a story like this from the perspective of the migrant, they develop a better understanding of what migrants go through. This process of reading the Bible through the lens of migrants then creates a space for migrants to process how they feel, and it creates a space for host communities to realize the significance of hospitality and integration. This interpretive process helps build an understanding of the fears of migrants and a recognition of how God is at work in meeting those needs through those who perceive themselves as host communities. Intercultural churches, then, are places where people are able to share with their brothers and sisters the anxieties that accompany migration and places where God manifests God's care and love to the alien through the hands of those who shepherd and welcome the lonely, the uprooted, and the fearful, providing them with blessings, comfort, and above all, a loving community.

The relationship between Isaac and the Philistines is challenged by Isaac's deception and by the envy of the Philistines when Isaac prospers in their midst. Isaac lies to the Philistines about the identity of his wife Rebecca (who is silent throughout the story), telling them that she is his sister. When the Philistines find out that she is indeed his wife, Isaac explains to them that he lied "because I thought I might die because of her" (26:9). This episode ends with the intriguing reversal in which the Philistines appear to be morally superior to Isaac. They explain to Isaac that he has no right to fear them and that the real threat is his deception (26:10–11). As the story develops, Isaac prospers in the land of the Philistines to the point that the Philistines start to see him as a threat. "The Philistines envied him" (26:14), and as a result, they asked him to leave: "Go away from us; you have become too powerful for us" (26:16).

It is evident in this story that fear of the other is what motivates deception and rejection. Isaac fears for his life, so he acts based on his prejudice about the Philistines, who initially welcomed him and protected him and his wife (26:11). The Philistines are afraid of Isaac because they are not sure how this migrant is going to use his wealth and power in their midst, especially given that he has lied to them about his wife. Deception and envy are motivated by fear of the other, which distorts the relationship between the sojourner and the host. It is noteworthy here that the well-being of the relationship between the migrant and the host is threatened by the way both sides have failed to know one another. Both sides are mutually responsible for the distortion of the relationship.

Therefore, restoration of the relationship starts with recognizing the mutuality of the migrant and the host as subjects who are capable of harming the relationship but also as subjects who are capable of reaching out to the other in order to restore the relationship. The Philistines express their hostility toward Isaac by filling with dirt the wells that his father Abraham had dug. Even though Isaac has become "too powerful," he does not use any violence to protect himself or to fulfill the divine promises. In the midst of this uncertainty, God appears to Isaac to assure him, "Do not be afraid, for I am with you" (26:24). Although the divine appearances and promises are mediated to Isaac, the Philistines are portrayed as a godly people who recognize the divine presence and act upon that recognition. Because God is with Isaac, the Philistines reach out to Isaac, whom they have earlier asked to leave, in order to establish a covenant. Here Isaac the migrant becomes the host as he prepares for them a feast of food and drink (26:30). Not only that, they also stay overnight and establish the covenant the next day. Building peace between the migrant and the host is grounded in the rejection of violence and in the recognition that the best way to deal with the fear of the other is to get to know others for who they are.[3]

With whom do readers of this story identify? Do readers who have settled in one country for generations identify with Isaac because they see themselves as the people of God? Would these readers identify with the Philistines? Do recent migrants and refugees identify with Isaac because he is a sojourner? Reading the Bible in an intercultural church requires reading the text from the perspective of the other and thinking about the ethical implications of behavior toward the other. Relationships in an intercultural church can be transformed if those who have settled for many generations in one place remember that the ancestors in the book of Genesis were migrants, so these readers need to remember their own stories of migration. Yet readers who have settled for a long time are more like the Philistines in the narrative and less like the ancestors, and they are called upon to show hospitality to the migrants who are accompanied by God. This process of reading unsettles those who constantly identify with the people of God because they want to claim the divine blessings and promises without reflecting on what it means to be a migrant and an alien resident.

For those who have recently experienced the anxieties of migration, these texts offer assurance that God is with them, God will bless them, and God will give them a sense of orientation, rootedness, and belonging to a community. José E. Ramírez Kidd suggests that the Israelites conceived of themselves as sojourners in order "to bring them under the direct protection of Yahweh." This designation "allowed them to transfer the hopes, formerly pinned on the land, to Yahweh. This absolute dependence on God empowered them to overcome the uncertainties and the sense of strangeness created by the possession of their land by foreigners."[4]

It is noticeable in this narrative that God works with and through both the host community and the migrant community. Forming an intercultural church calls for people who settled a long time ago to welcome migrants, help them integrate, and not fear their prosperity. At the same time, as the divine promises pronounced in this narrative assure and comfort the migrant in the midst of the fear and trauma of displacement, the divine promises also hold the migrants accountable for the well-being of those who host them and welcome them, lest they themselves forget that they are migrants living by the promise.

The Church as Community of Sojourners: A Perspective from the New Testament

In the New Testament, the church is addressed as a community of sojourners and resident aliens. Examples that are especially pertinent can be found in 1 Peter and Hebrews.

1 Peter

In the opening words of the epistle of 1 Peter, the text identifies the audience of this letter as "the exiles of the Dispersion in Pontus, Galatia, Cappadocia, Asia, and Bithynia, who have been chosen and destined by God the Father and sanctified by the Spirit to be obedient to Jesus Christ and to be sprinkled with his blood: May grace and peace be yours in abundance." While the New Revised Standard Version captures the meaning of this greeting, the English translation rearranges the Greek words to fit English syntax better. In the Greek text, the word *eklektois* ("the elected ones") comes right before the description of the addressee as "the exiles of the dispersion" (*parepidēmois diasporas*). Such a description holds in tension two facets of the identity of the people who are addressed by the author: they are simultaneously elected by God and sojourners living in diaspora.

Interpreters of 1 Peter have pondered the meaning of the description of the recipients of the epistle as "the exiles of the Dispersion" in 1:1 or as "aliens and exiles" in 2:11 (see also 1:17). Should the readers of 1 Peter understand this description literally or metaphorically? Interpreters who take this description in its literal sense suggest that Peter is addressing Christians from a Jewish background, who as residents of Asia Minor not only occupied the fringes of the society but also lacked legal rights because they were not citizens. To those who are in diaspora and have no legal standing, the author makes the case that they can now in Christ be members of a community and enjoy the privilege of being part of the house of God: "Once you were not a people, but now you are God's people" (2:10).[5]

Another approach understands the description of the audience of the epistle as exiles and aliens in a metaphorical sense. Peter is addressing gentiles who have legal status in Asia Minor, yet he calls them aliens and sojourners in order to signify their new identity as Christians, who should alienate themselves from the world. The author subverts the negative reality of being aliens and exiles, which usually describes people who hold no rights, and turns the image on its head to invite these Christians to claim social alienation as a unique identity given to them by God.[6]

Benjamin Dunning suggests a third approach to understanding the description of Christians as aliens and sojourners. Given that the author of 1 Peter also urges the Christians to engage with the social and political structures around them, Dunning argues that "the text marks Christian identity as distinctive by figuring Christians as outsiders to the social order, while simultaneously engaging in a paraenetic agenda that serves to reinscribe their place in that social order."[7] Dunning here highlights the tension that surrounds the identity of the Christian community, which sees itself as an outsider to the world but at the same time seeks to transform the world that surrounds it.

It is interesting to note that the ambiguity of the social location of the audience of the letter of Peter has parallels in the the varied social locations of Christian communities that read the epistle nowadays. Some readers of the epistle are migrants and refugees who are going through literal experiences of being in diaspora, while other readers are citizens of host countries to which migrants and refugees flee. Reading the Bible through the lens of migrant communities and through the lens of settled communities calls for further reflection on Peter's description of the recipients as both "aliens" and "chosen."

As I showed earlier in this chapter, in the Hebrew Bible, the identity of the faith community as sojourners is qualified by receiving promises from God and vice versa. That is, as the faith community becomes grounded in a particular time and space, its members should not forget they are temporary residents. Here, too, in 1 Peter, in the three places where the text describes the audience as "the exiles of the Dispersion," ones experiencing a "time of . . . exile," and "aliens and exiles" (1:1, 17; 2:11), the text also proclaims divine promises that describe the other side of the identity of the faith community. First, the exiles of the Dispersion are addressed as chosen ones (1:1). It is likely that Peter is drawing from the book of Isaiah this theological claim of God choosing the exiles. While the people were in exile away from their homeland, God addressed them as God's chosen servant: "for the sake of my servant Jacob, and Israel my chosen" (Isa 45:4). Peter used the Greek word *eklektos* ("chosen"), which is the same word the Septuagint[8] uses to translate the Hebrew word *bḥr* ("to elect"; see also Isa 65:9; Ps 105:6). In times of hopelessness and despair for the exile, election, which signifies a secure divine commitment to God's people, functioned as an anchor of hope in the face of the oppression and alienation of the empire.

Through God's steadfast love, the "exiles" are born again into a living hope through the resurrection of Jesus Christ for an eternal inheritance (1 Peter 1:3–4). In addition to calling them "chosen" at the opening of the letter, the author urges them to "live in reverent fear during the time of your exile" (1:17). Those who are described as living in a time of exile (*paroikias*) are called to live by the fear of the Lord because God is an impartial parent. For those who experience exile in its literal or metaphorical sense, who feel alienated or abandoned by family, God becomes their parent, and they are God's children (1:14, 17). Those who feel uprooted, the author plants in the history of the people of God in the Hebrew Bible by urging them to be holy because God is holy (1:15–16; Lev 19:1–2). While the culture of the market values people based on their productivity, the value of these sojourners cannot be measured by the silver and gold of the world, because they were ransomed by the priceless blood of Christ (1 Peter 1:18; cf. Mark 10:45; Exod 6:6; Isa 43:1).

Finally, the third place where the author addresses the audience as "aliens and exiles" (1 Peter 2:11) comes right after a foundational theological claim that binds the church as living stones to the cornerstone, Jesus Christ (2:4–10). While Jesus was rejected by people, he was chosen (*eklektos*) by God (2:4). Although the exiles are alienated and estranged by their surrounding culture and systems, the author says they "are a chosen race, a royal priesthood, a holy nation, God's own people" (2:9). In this way, the author incorporates these strangers and exiles into the people of God (Exod 19:5–6; Hos 1:6–10). As God's people, they have a mission to "proclaim the mighty acts of God," who transferred them "out of darkness into [God's] marvelous light" (1 Peter 2:9). Though they are sojourners, they are called to become agents of change.

Shively Smith, after critiquing the abuse of 1 Peter by slave owners to justify slavery in America, makes the case that the identity of the church as a diaspora or a sojourning community testifies to the divine activity that is at work renewing the church:

> Diaspora is not punishment for followers of Christ but reward for their unwavering commitment to the practices and basic beliefs of Christianity. First Peter's diaspora . . . is an essential feature of Christian confession and community. Diaspora, in the letter, represents not the destruction of a people but the making of a new, more pluralistic and tolerant kinship. . . . It inaugurates the constitution of a new and unconventional fellowship (*koinōneō*, 1 Pet 4:13) composed of mixed ethnic, territorial, and cultural backgrounds.[9]

If the surrounding culture seeks to build walls of fear to separate peoples from each other, the sojourning people of God are called to show hospitality to one another and to use the gifts that God has given them to serve others (4:10–11). Whether the community experiences exile because they are literally migrants or because they are alienated by the society due to their ethical commitments, God announces promises that empower them to persevere in the face of pain and suffering. The dual citizenship of members of the sojourning house of God forms their ethical decisions and how they ought to live in this world.

Hebrews

The author of the epistle to the Hebrews also addresses Christians as a community of resident aliens and sojourners:

> All of these died in faith without having received the promises, but from a distance they saw and greeted them. They confessed that they were strangers and foreigners on the earth, for people who speak in this way make it clear that they are seeking a homeland. If they had been thinking of the land that they had left behind, they would have had opportunity to return. But as it is, they desire a better country, that is, a heavenly one. Therefore, God is not ashamed to be called their God; indeed, he has prepared a city for them. (Heb 11:13–16)

The author of Hebrews interrupts the sequence of the faith heroes in order to explain the reason why these ancestors lived such a life full of faith. Needless to say, the author of Hebrews does not get into the failures of these ancestors. Rather, the author shows how central this idea of being aliens and sojourners was to the formation of the faith of the ancestors. They called themselves aliens and sojourners because they knew they belonged to another home, which their God was preparing for them. Not only were they aliens, but they also lived by their faith in God, who promised to be faithful. The church is called to live by faith, claiming its identity as a community of sojourners whose home country is being called God's people. The promises are never completely fulfilled here and now; therefore, the life of faith is about trusting in God's word and promise. This faith is tried here and now, sometimes through challenges that test whether the church is capable of behaving ethically in a way that reflects its trust in God. Those tests of faith occur not when the church isolates itself from the world but rather when it engages the world.

For the sake of my discussion here, to be alien is not to be called to be separated from the world. Equally important, being connected with the world should be shaped and transformed by the other side of the reality of the Christian identity—namely, that they belong to another home and that being aliens demands that they live in a way that reflects the sacrificial love that has made them members of this heavenly home. Stanley Hauerwas and William Willimon write, "We would like a church that again asserts that God, not nations, rules the world, that the boundaries of God's kingdom transcend those of Caesar, and that the main political task of the church is the formation of people who see clearly the cost of discipleship and are willing to pay the price."[10]

> The church is called to live by faith, claiming its identity as a community of sojourners.

Separationist ecclesiology has the tendency to idealize the church and to demonize the world. In the stories I previously cited from Genesis, those who might be considered outsiders (Hittites and Philistines) showed goodness to the ancestors of Israel. Separationist ecclesiology helps minorities preserve their identity, but it tends to alienate them from seeking their civic rights in the society. Separationist ecclesiology might shelter main-culture or privileged Christians from supporting those who are suffering economically or socially. Separationist ecclesiology, however, plays a significant role in forming disciples who recognize that the real change lies in God's power and happens through the commitment of the faithful disciples to the kingdom of God. Many of the readers of the New Testament read the text from the perspective of a settled community that has historical roots where they currently live. Such a social location can lead to the neutralization of the identity of the addressees as sojourners and aliens, and focus on the spiritualization of Christian identity. Neutralization or spiritualization affects the memory of what it means to be a migrant or an outsider who occupies the periphery.

Recognizing that Christians are called to be aliens unsettles the sense of being at the center, and it opens the mind and heart of the community to those who experience literal marginalization. Reclaiming the identity of migrants is not meant to hijack the actual experience of people who were forced to migrate, nor is it an attempt to belittle the experience of alienation that others literally experience in our midst. And it is not an attempt to release those who hold the privilege of being citizens from their responsibility toward the migrant, the refugee, and the alien. The intention behind claiming the identity of the Christian community as sojourners is to remind Christians of their ultimate citizenship as members of the people of God and to exhort them to develop empathy toward those who are alienated or marginalized because they are migrants or undocumented.

By recognizing otherness as intrinsic to what it means to be a church, the faith community is called to deconstruct the centralization of one culture as the heart of the identity of the church. The church is called to construct new ways of offering worship, experiencing fellowship, and being witnesses by being open to different practices and expressions of the Christian faith. That harmony has yet to be a reality in the city that God is preparing should not be a reason to put off striving to live up to this reality here and now. Like the ancestors, the church is called to live by faith and take steps forward toward this reality that is guaranteed by God. When the church lives out this life of faith, it embodies an alternative to the cultures that are torn apart because of fear, hatred, and sinful claims of supremacy.

Integration and Justice

The story of Joseph as found in Genesis 37–50 is a novella of a forced migrant. Forced migration resulted from favoritism, hatred, and fear of abuse of power that dominated the politics of his family of origin. Thrown into the pit and then sold into slavery by his own brothers, the youngster Joseph finds himself in a foreign land that he did not know before. In Egypt, Joseph shows resilience in the face of trauma. Because the Lord is with him and because of his hard work, his master, Potiphar, makes him supervisor over all of Potiphar's house. But because he is a migrant, Joseph is not granted a hearing when Potiphar's wife accuses Joseph of rape; instead, he is thrown into prison (Genesis 39).

In prison, Joseph interprets dreams, an ability that leads him to excel in Egypt, where he is an alien or sojourner. His life is transformed because he interprets the dreams of Pharaoh. Pharaoh rewards Joseph's wise interpretations by appointing him as his second man in command. Despite all of his hardships, Joseph is able to save not only the land of Egypt but also his own family from famine. It is evident from his clothing and his marriage to an Egyptian woman that Joseph has assimilated into the Egyptian culture, yet he maintains a Hebrew identity, which is evident in the names he gives to his children (Genesis 41).

His whole family of origin moves to Egypt at the generous command of Pharaoh and forms a separate identity by living in Goshen. Still, their shared identity as Egyptians and Hebrews is evident in the rituals that accompany the burial of Joseph's father, Jacob: he is mummified according to the Egyptian customs but buried in a cave in Canaan with his ancestors (Genesis 50). When Joseph reconciles with his brothers, he is able to forgive them because he understands his hardship to be part of a divine plan to save his family (Genesis 45). Thus, the story of Joseph offers many insights into the life of migrants and into the process of forming intercultural communities. But for the sake of the discussion here, I will focus on two episodes that offer cautionary tales around migration, integration, and the importance of justice for building intercultural societies and churches.

In Potiphar's House

Joseph's first encounter with Egyptian culture takes place in Potiphar's house. The narrator leaves no room for speculation about the Lord's involvement in the life of Joseph: "The Lord was with Joseph, and he became a successful man" (Gen 39:2). The Lord was present with the forced migrant. When people are betrayed by their kin and forced to migrate, God becomes their friend, companion, and family. The Lord's presence in Egypt with Joseph makes him a successful man. According to the narrator, Joseph's success as a result of the Lord's blessing is also noticed by his Egyptian master. The foreigner here is portrayed as person who can recognize the Lord's hand and blessing. This awareness builds a relationship of trust between Joseph and Potiphar: "Joseph found favor in his sight and attended him; he made him overseer of his house and put him in charge of all that he had" (39:3–4). As a result, the Lord blesses the house of Potiphar because of Joseph; the blessing is comprehensive in that it reaches everything that Potiphar has in the house and in the field (39:5–6).

In this episode, the non-Hebrew Egyptian man is the host who has spiritual capacities to recognize the work of the Lord in the migrant. Joseph, the Hebrew, who is in a foreign land, is a recipient of the hospitality of the host community. The categories are fuzzy here: from an Egyptian perspective, Joseph is the foreigner; from the perspective of the narrative, Joseph is the Hebrew insider and Potiphar is the outsider. In any case, forced migrants are looking for opportunities to succeed and undo the traumatic experiences they are going through. Host communities can create hospitable spaces for migrants to prosper. Forced migrants who have experienced the trauma of leaving everything behind and encountering a new and unfamiliar culture need to be seen as equal and valuable human beings. Because of Joseph's success, he is integrated into Potiphar's household and granted power. Joseph is not seen as a threat. Yet this integration is questioned: Will the Egyptians treat Joseph as a human being who is worthy of justice? Or is Joseph only seen as an economic asset?

Joseph's status as an integrated migrant is tested when he is accused of rape. When Potiphar's wife tries to have Joseph lie down with her, he refuses because he honors his master's trust and because this would be a sin against God (39:8–9). When another attempt to entice him fails, Potiphar's wife accuses Joseph of trying to rape her. The way she describes her version of the story to the people of the house and to her husband highlights the fact that Joseph is a slave and a Hebrew: "The Hebrew servant, whom you have brought among us, came in to me to insult me" (39:17; see also 39:14). Potiphar's wife's narrative highlights the differences between herself and Joseph. She is a rich Egyptian woman, while he is a male Hebrew slave. Joseph's initial integration into Potiphar's household is now threatened and all wonder whether justice will be done. Will Potiphar give Joseph a hearing?

While Potiphar's wife gets to tell her story twice to two different audiences, Joseph's voice is silenced. The narrator highlights this distinction by actually repeating her words and narrative. Joseph is not granted justice, and his version of the story is not heard. We can compare Joseph's story with an Egyptian story of two brothers, in which a certain brother is accused by his sister-in-law of rape. In that story, the accused brother's voice is heard, and the lie is exposed. This comparison shows that Joseph is deprived of justice because of his sociopolitical status as a Hebrew slave. While the host community at first received and was blessed by Joseph, the same community also treats Joseph as an object. When he resists, he is deprived of justice.

In an intercultural society and church, the nobility of the motif of integration will be questioned: Are migrants and the "culturally other" people welcomed only because they are a source of a blessing? Are people welcomed in the church because they will revive the church and increase its numbers? Indeed, migrants can be a blessing, but will they be granted justice when lies about them spread or when they resist being turned into an object to be consumed by the dominant culture? To be sure, God desires to bless both migrant and host communities. Although human actions might hinder the mutuality of these blessings, God continues to interfere to direct the course of the events. This narrative is a cautionary tale around

> God desires to bless both migrant and host communities.

the motif for integration. It reminds us that integration needs to follow the path of justice, even if it is costly, and the path of truth that exposes lies and stereotypes that seek to exclude the vulnerable.

Egyptians Enslaved in Their Own Land

In the preceding episode (Genesis 39), the integration of the migrant did not adequately address the issue of justice for the outsider. In another episode in the Joseph narrative, the question of integration and justice is raised but from the other end of the relationship—namely, what happens when the migrant possesses power: Will the migrant (Joseph) work for justice and liberty for the Egyptians, or will the migrant buy into the economic systems that centralize money and wealth in the hands of those who are already privileged?

Joseph, now in his role as an Egyptian ruler, encounters his brothers, and makes them go through all that he experienced. He then reveals his identity after he sees glimpses of their transformation (Genesis 42–44). When Pharaoh hears that Joseph has a family, he generously offers to host them in Goshen, the best part of the land of Egypt (Gen 45:16–28). Upon their arrival in Egypt, Jacob meets Pharaoh and offers him a blessing, and Pharaoh in turn invites them to work for him as shepherds of his cattle (Gen 47:1–10). Then the text notes that "Joseph settled his father and his brothers, and granted them a holding in the land of Egypt, in the best part of the land, in the land of Rameses, as Pharaoh had instructed. And Joseph provided his father, his brothers, and all his father's household with food, according to the number of their dependents" (Gen 47:11–12). Following this is the episode that reports Joseph enslaving the Egyptian people for his ruler Pharaoh (47:13–26).

The episode begins with the report that there was no food in Egypt and Canaan. The people have no silver to buy more grain to eat and survive because Joseph has already collected their money in exchange for food and given it to Pharaoh. With no money left and food running out, the Egyptian people come to Joseph, pleading, "Give us food! Why should we die before your eyes? For our money is gone" (47:15). Joseph then asks them to bring all of their cattle in order to buy food (47:16–17). When the people finish the food given to them for that year, they have nothing to give to Joseph to buy grain other than their lands and their bodies, so Joseph buys their land for Pharaoh (47:18–21). The priests are exempted from this practice (47:22). Then, Joseph makes a deal with the people, since they and their lands are possessed by Pharaoh: Joseph will give them seeds to plant the land, and they will give one-fifth of the crops to Pharaoh. The remaining four-fifths they will keep as food and as seeds for the land (47:23–24). The narrator reports a very curious statement pronounced by the Egyptians who have just been turned into slaves: "You have saved our lives; may it please my lord, we will be slaves to Pharaoh" (47:25). The Egyptians are caught between death by famine and enslavement to Pharaoh.

Although this episode does not seem to be an original part of the story of Joseph, it still teaches important lessons about migration, integration, and justice. The story does not seem to fit the original Joseph narrative because the way it handles the crisis of the famine differs from the original plan that Joseph suggested to Pharaoh in Genesis 41:33–36. Furthermore, Joseph earlier told his brothers that they needed to move to Egypt because the famine was so severe that they still would have five years of no farming or harvest (Gen 45:6). Note also that the Egyptians seem to have good relationships with Joseph in Genesis 50:3, 11, which is evident in their weeping over Jacob when he dies. Interpreters of the story suggest that this episode was added to the Joseph narrative in order to explain the Egyptian practice of gathering one-fifth of the crops into Pharaoh's house. At any rate, this narrative is a cautionary tale that shows how migrants who prosper in their new context can also fall into oppressive economic practices that deprive natives of the resources to prosper.[11] Joseph, the migrant, uses his power to serve the power structures in Egypt at the expense of the people. While the family of Joseph and Jacob received food and land from Joseph and Pharaoh, the Egyptians have to sell themselves and their land so that they will survive.

The story of Joseph is a rich narrative that addresses issues around cross-cultural relations between migrant and host communities. The episode of Joseph's experience in Potiphar's house and the episode of the enslavement of the Egyptians show that integration and justice must go hand in hand. The hospitality of communities to the migrant and the migrant's prosperity in the land of migration are tested by opportunities to show or deny justice for the other. For integration to endure, host and migrant communities must persist in walking the path of truth, justice, equality, and mutuality. This path is costly and requires self-criticism and a willingness to confront one's own tendencies to secure personal well-being at the expense of the other. This hard work, however, brings divine blessings to host and migrant communities who look after the marginalized and the oppressed.

Sojourn, Empathy, and Justice

Becoming an intercultural church or society is not just a matter of embracing diversity. Claiming the identity of migrant and sojourner calls for doing justice. The legal texts of the Old Testament repeatedly exhort the Israelites to act justly toward alien residents, those who do not have a family system that would empower them in courts. The ethical formation of a people capable of showing justice to the marginalized is grounded in four aspects in the legal material. These include memory, empathy, loving oneself, and imitating God.

Quite often, this call for legal and economic justice to the resident alien is grounded in the fact that the Israelites themselves were sojourners and resident aliens in Egypt. In the Book of the Covenant (Exodus 21-23), God exhorts the people, "You shall not wrong or oppress a resident alien, for you were aliens in the land of Egypt" (Exod 22:21). The text goes on to proclaim, "You shall not oppress a resident alien; you know the heart of an alien, for you were aliens in the land of Egypt" (Exod 23:9). The

Hebrew word *lakhats* ("to oppress") is the same word that is used to describe the experience of the Hebrew slaves who were oppressed by the Egyptian taskmasters (Exod 3:9). That is, the law is calling for fair and just treatment of the alien because the Israelites know well the cruelty of oppression and humiliation.

Memory

What happens when citizens or legal residents of a host country remember that at some point in their history, they or their ancestors immigrated or were forced to migrate? What is lost when this aspect of their story is ignored or erased from memory? When people ignore or forget about their migration history and only cling to the fact that they are lawful citizens, they bury a significant part of their story. They bury the stories of when their ancestors immigrated, were forced to migrate, or invaded another people's land. Burying these aspects of the stories because they are painful or shameful, or dismissing them because they seem irrelevant in a new political system, can block out the ability to welcome the stranger. Memory plays an active role in forming people as moral agents, because it reminds people that the stranger is not out there but within, close to them, a part of who they are, and a central aspect of their story.

Empathy

Remembering personal and communal stories of movement and migration can spark compassion and empathy toward the migrant, the sojourner, the alien, the undocumented, and the refugee. Leviticus 19:33–34 says, "When an alien resides with you in your land, you shall not oppress the alien. The alien who resides with you shall be to you as the citizen among you; you shall love the alien as yourself, for you were aliens in the land of Egypt: I am the Lord your God." Simply put, empathy is "feeling what someone else feels" or "imagining oneself in another's situation."[12] Amy Coplan's study *Understanding Empathy* suggests that there are "three essential features of empathy: affective matching, other-oriented perspective-taking, and self-other differentiation."[13] For empathy to happen, one person "must experience affective states that are qualitatively the same as those of" the other.[14] Empathy is different, however, from emotional contagion in that empathy is mediated and "requires perspective-taking."[15]

Scholars who study empathy differentiate between self-perspective taking and other-perspective taking. The former looks into what the self would feel if it were in a particular situation, while the latter recognizes and imitates how the other feels in that situation. The critical distinction here is that the self does not impose its perspective on the other. Imagine someone lost a job that they were ready to quit. A self-perspective empathy from someone who had lost a job and was sad about it might imagine that the other person is sad, while an other-perspective empathy might express readiness for a new beginning. Other-perspective taking when coupled with "self-other differentiation" helps "not only to prevent ourselves from losing sight of the other as an other, but also prevents us from losing our awareness of our own selves as separate agents."[16] This last point here has important implications for the church as it seeks to do justice for migrants. The ability to differentiate between self and other in showing empathy allows settled communities to think about how the alien and foreigner experience their migration process, and at the same time, it helps the empathizing community, one hopes, to be aware of their privilege so that even when they act as allies with the alien and stranger, they listen to how the migrants want to tell their own stories.

Loving Self, Loving Other

People will be capable of loving the foreigner when they come to terms with their own stories of migration. The text exhorts the people to "love the alien as yourself." This basically binds the love of self with the love of the alien resident. Quite often, humans try to constitute their identity over against the other or away from the other, but from God's perspective, constructing one's identity or loving oneself is connected to how one treats the alien, the other. God reminds the people that loving the stranger as oneself is connected to remembering their own story as ones who were once aliens in Egypt. Being in touch with one's story deepens one's self-understanding and therefore enables one to relate to the other in a way that reflects being reconciled with one's identity as a sojourner. When the people were sojourners, they were longing for freedom, dignity, hospitality, and a sense of belonging. If this is what it meant to love oneself, then loving the alien as oneself means offering dignity, freedom, hospitality, and a home to the stranger. This kind of love flows from empathy, and empathy can be deepened by what we remember.

Imitating God

The divine command to treat the alien with equality is grounded in the covenant between God and the people: "I am the LORD your God" (Lev 19:34). The commandments that precede "I am the LORD your God" are not a matter of preference or choice on the people's part; the people are bound to these ethical standards as partners with God in the covenant. The text exhorts the people of Israel to deal justly with the alien who resides in their midst. Justice in these verses is expressed both negatively and positively. Not only must the Israelites not mistreat the alien, they must treat the alien as a citizen with equal rights and responsibilities. Equality is granted to the alien without regard to their race, ethnicity, color, or religious background.

Interestingly, Deuteronomy connects the just treatment of the alien with God's love. In words similar to those of Leviticus, Deuteronomy commands the people to love the stranger because they themselves were strangers in Egypt (10:19). But before that, Deuteronomy makes it clear that God "loves" the strangers, and as a manifestation of this love, God provides for them: "For the LORD your God is God of gods and LORD of lords, the great God, mighty and awesome, who is not partial and takes no bribe, who executes justice for the orphan and the widow, and who loves the strangers, providing them food and clothing" (Deut 10:17–18). That is, when the people are exhorted to love the stranger, they are called to imitate God. God's greatness, might, power, and awesomeness are manifested in showing compassion to the powerless and the oppressed. The church that understands the character of God and seeks to imitate God uses its power and privilege for the sake of the alien and poor. The work of justice for strangers and aliens should start with loving them as God does, and loving the strangers can be sparked by remembering and telling the stories of our own strangeness and alienation.

> The work of justice for strangers and aliens should start with loving them as God does.

Memory, empathy, loving oneself, and imitating God, who loves the stranger, are central to forming a community that seeks the justice and the well-being of migrants and refugees. An intercultural church that creates a space for the memory of sojourning to form its members morally will not only advocate for justice outside the church in the society and along the border but also embody this love for the stranger. Further, it will live these just relationships in its own governing by giving leadership roles to members who come from less-dominant cultures. It will integrate unfamiliar ways of worship, fellowship, and ministry in order to live up to its diverse theologies and spiritualties. An important step toward doing justice for the migrant and the alien in and outside the church can be taken when the migrant and the host communities come to the belief that each community needs the other, and each community has something to offer the other.

Discussion Questions

1. In what way is reading the Bible through the eyes of migrants disorienting and destabilizing?

2. In what ways does reading the Bible help recenter or reorient sojourning or migrant peoples?

3. In what ways were Abraham and other ancestors of the Israelites sojourners or aliens? How and why was this also true for the New Testament churches?

4. For centuries, the Christian church was the dominant institution of faith in Western society. In the United States, the mainline Protestant and Roman Catholic churches have held a central place in our culture. In what ways do you see this changing today? How might the images of sojourner and alien apply to churches or communities of faith in today's world?

5. Review the story of Isaac with the Philistines in Genesis 26 (see pp. 51–56). Who is the sojourner (alien) in the story, and who is the host resident? With whom do you identify and why? How and when do the roles reverse?

6. What particular fears or anxieties do migrants or aliens face when entering a new land? Have you ever felt like a sojourner or alien? Describe the experience and the emotions you felt.

7. On p. 65, the author states, "The intention behind claiming the identity of the Christian community as sojourners is to remind Christians of their ultimate citizenship as members of the people of God and to exhort them

to develop empathy toward those who are alienated or marginalized." How does citizenship in the people of God differ from citizenship in one's country? How does one develop or show empathy for the alienated or marginalized as individuals, nation, or church)?

8. How do the roles of sojourner or alien and ruler or host play out in the story of Joseph in Genesis 37–50? Talk about how the roles shift, especially for Joseph.

9. What role do memory, empathy, loving self and other, and imitating God play in creating a true intercultural church?

3

Worship and the Intercultural Reality of the Church

One of the central migration stories in the Bible is found in the book of Exodus. The people of Israel do not just leave Egypt and march toward the land of the promise, they also move from oppression to freedom. God's liberating salvation is not just about what they are liberated from but also about what they are liberated into. In Hebrew, the same root ʿbd could mean "to serve" or "to worship." In their experience of oppression, the people were enslaved in servitude (ʿbd) to Pharaoh (Exod 1:13–14), but in God's liberating vision, the people were to leave Egypt so that they would worship (ʿbd) God in the wilderness (Exod 7:16; 8:1). Exodus, as a story of migration, shows that God's mission in the world is to liberate people from a culture of oppression in order to form a worshipping community.

A culture of oppression results from the absence of being in relationship and a lack of knowledge of the other. Initially, the Egyptian pharaoh in Genesis shows hospitality to Jacob's family on account of Joseph, the forced migrant who saved Egypt from the famine. Pharaoh even gives them some of the best land in the kingdom. But as the book of Exodus opens, the new pharaoh oppresses the descendants of Jacob because he does not know Joseph (Exod 1:8). Lack of relationship and absence of the knowledge of the other leaves a vacuum for fear to take over. Moved by fear of the Israelites, whose population is increasing, Pharaoh decides to deal shrewdly with them, lest they join in war against Egypt. Pharaoh's plan then is to turn the Israelites into his slaves. God's response to this culture of fear and oppression is to form a liberated worshipping community.

A Worshipping Community as God's Mission

Reflecting on the relation between mission and worship, theologian Thomas Schattauer argues that there are at least three models for understanding how worship relates to mission: "inside and out" (conventional), "outside in" (contemporary), and "inside out" (radically traditional). In the first model, worship is an activity that takes place inside the church, and mission is an activity that takes place outside of the church. The goal of worship is to nurture the faith community so that the faithful will go out and do their missional activities. Worship indirectly serves mission. The second model brings the "outside" activities of mission more directly into the context of worship, either by preaching the gospel to the unchurched and irreligious or by rallying commitment for social and political action. Worship is a direct instrument for mission. Schattauer argues for something different:

> There is a third way—inside out. This approach locates the liturgical assembly itself within the arena of the *missio Dei* ("the mission of God"). The *missio Dei* is God's own movement outward in relation to the world—in creation and the covenant with Israel and culminating in Jesus Christ and the community gathered in him. . . . From this perspective, there is no separation between liturgy and mission. . . . The relationship between worship and mission is not instrumental, either directly or indirectly, but rather the assembly for worship is mission.[1]

I believe that Exodus 3:1–12, which is known as the call of Moses, makes the point that forming a worshipping community is God's mission in the world. When God commissions Moses to liberate the Israelites from Egypt, Moses immediately protests, "Who am I that I should go to Pharaoh, and bring the Israelites out of Egypt?" (3:11). God responds to him by saying, "I will be with you; and this shall be the sign for you that it is I who sent you: when you have brought the people out of Egypt, you shall worship God on this mountain" (3:12). One wonders: how is this supposed to be a sign? "Ordinarily," writes Brevard Childs, "a sign takes the form of a concrete guarantee which follows the promise and yet precedes the fulfillment."[2] But this sign would only confirm the word after the mission had been accomplished.

Because this is an unusual sign, some commentators have suggested that the demonstrative (Heb. *zeh*, Eng. *this* in Exod 3:12) is referring to the preceding clause: "I will be with you." Yahweh's companionship with Moses will be the sign that Yahweh has sent him. The problem with this interpretation is that the demonstrative usually refers to what is mentioned after it and not to what is mentioned before it.

The other option, then, is that the demonstrative refers to what follows: "the people would worship Yahweh on the same mountain after the successful deliverance from Egypt."[3] Grammatically speaking, this is the most plausible suggestion. Therefore, the sign of God's liberating mission in the world is that there is an assembled community that offers worship. This is the first sign mentioned in the book, before Moses turns the rod into a snake or the water into blood. A worshipping community is the miracle, the sign! A worshipping community is the sign of God's activity in this world. The wordplay between the burning bush, *seneh*, and the name of the mountain where they will worship, Sinai, invites us to consider that there is connection between the divine appearance to Moses in the burning-but-not-consumed bush and the theophany (God's appearance) in the midst of the people on the mountain in the form of fire, where God proclaims to the people, "Indeed, the whole earth is mine, but you shall be for me a priestly kingdom and a holy nation" (Exod 19:5–6).

> A worshipping community is the sign of God's activity in this world.

The formation of a worshipping community is an essential aspect of God's liberating mission is evident in the fact that God calls the people a "priestly kingdom," a description that the New Testament writers extend to include the church (see the discussion of Rev 5:9–10 later in this chapter), pointing to an office that mediates between God and the world in rituals and worship. Furthermore, while leaving Egypt behind occupies the first section of the book of Exodus (chaps. 1–18), a large portion of Exodus is dedicated to building the tabernacle (Exodus 25–30; 35–40), which enables the people to worship God, who is present in their midst. Therefore, it is safe to say that the mission of God is not just about liberating the people *from* slavery but also about liberating the people *into* worship of God.

The recent global wave of migration confronts the church with a need to reread the exodus narrative as a migration story in which the people of God as a worshipping community leave behind cultures of fear and segregation in order to experience God's liberating power to build intercultural worshipping communities that embody the politics of hospitality to the other. Through the passage of baptism, the church commits itself to God's liberating mission of forming a worshipping community, and through the Lord's Supper, God sustains the unity and the diversity of the church as it journeys through the wilderness of this world (1 Cor 10:1–4). If political discourse nowadays is centered on xenophobic fear of the migrant, and if political discourse calls for building walls to keep the oppressed and vulnerable outside, then envisioning a communal worship that welcomes the migrant and builds bridges of trust between cultural expressions of faith becomes a form of resistance to imperial domination.

Worship and Culture

Being an intercultural church requires a bold vision that recognizes the challenges of the reality without letting the obstacles hinder the community from worshipping together. Being an intercultural church here and now should be inspired by the eschatological vision of Revelation 4–7, in which all believers from every tribe, language, and nation come together to offer their doxology, lament, and praise before God and the Lamb. In the midst of suffering and persecution, the author of Revelation follows the style of apocalyptic literature in order to empower the church to stand firm in the face of their current struggles. The author seeks to reveal to his audience the meaning of the unsettling reality they are experiencing. The final word, asserts the author, is that the beast, or the imperial rulers or the religious authorities, may seem to be in control, but they are not. Rather, God is enthroned, and the slaughtered Lamb holds all authority. The kingdom of God is present in the world, and the church is called to persevere in its faith in God in the face of the empire. This resilient faith is reflected in the church's costly act of worship and witness. Worshipping as a diverse faith community is a realization of the eschatological vision of the church that counters the reality of segregation, racism, and cultural supremacy.

The genre of Revelation calls the faith community to be imaginative and not to define reality by what is here and what is seen and what is present. The church is called to define reality by what is hoped for in God. The current reality is that the church is divided and segregated. The current state of affairs of the church and society is that it is polarized, and there is a growing sense of alienation and animosity. An intercultural church is an alternate reality. It is a form of active resistance to the status quo.

Worship Is about God

It might be worth stating the obvious. Worship is about God. God must be at the center of any theology or practice of worship. God's centrality frees humans from fighting and struggling over whose culture or whose way of worship is at the center of the act of worship. Now, this assertion does not mean that people should abandon their cultural articulation of faith or cultural praxis of worship. After all, worship is always expressed by a worshipping community that is located in time and space and expressed through words, thoughts, and bodily performances

> God's centrality liberates those who are fixed on their own culture and way of worship.

that are rooted in particular traditions. God's centrality liberates those who are fixed on their own culture and way of worship by reminding them that worship is not about them, but rather it is focused on God. Similarly, God's centrality liberates those who do not feel at home in a culture by showing them that God embraces all of God's people who come from different linguistic and ethnic backgrounds.

As I will demonstrate later in this chapter, in the visions of Revelation 4–7, the different peoples maintain what is unique about them—their language, tribal affiliation, ethnicity, and culture. Yet, the starting point for an intercultural church is to remember that God is calling the church first and above all to become a worshipping community centered on God. The series of visions does not begin with the dragon, or the empire, or the struggles of the faith community; rather, it starts with the affirmation that all things are under God's control, and it defines worship as the right human response to the proclamation of what God and the Lamb are doing for the sake of the marginalized faith community.

In the first scene from Revelation 4, John encounters a marvelous God who is enthroned in the heavens, looks like jasper and carnelian, and is surrounded by a rainbow, flashes of lightning, the sound of thunder, burning torches, and a sea of glass (4:2–6). Seated around the throne are twenty-four elders dressed in white and wearing golden crowns on their heads (4:4). These elders represent the twelve tribes and the twelve apostles, who together symbolize God's people. Around the throne are also four living creatures (lion, ox, human face, and eagle). These creatures represent all creation: the lion represents the wild, the ox represents domestic animals, the eagle represents the birds, and the human face represents the human species (4:6–8).

The author also appropriates images of rainbow, fire, and animals from Ezekiel 1. When God appears to Ezekiel in Babylon, the visions of God assert the sovereignty of God over the chaos of exile and underline hope in the midst of despair because the divine mobility allows God to accompany the exiles (see Ezek 11:16). Here in the setting of the book of Revelation, the author proclaims that it is God and not Caesar, the Roman emperor, who is the sovereign one. Mitchell Reddish underscores the importance of the throne vision: "By emphasizing the throne, John is pulling back the curtain and showing his readers the true locus of the world's power. The emperor may sit on his throne in Rome, but his throne is no match for God's throne. In spite of his lofty claims and grandiose pronouncements, the emperor is not in control of the universe. That power resides with God."[4] This vision of the enthroned God calls the reader to respond. Reddish adds, "Revelation demands a choice on the part of the reader. One must choose before whose throne one will bow. For John, the answer is simple. Because God is the one before whom all other powers must fall, only God is worthy of human worship, adoration, and praise."[5] For John, the four creatures and the twenty-four elders exemplify the right response to God's majesty when they offer worship to the one who is worthy.

The doxology proclaims that God is worthy of worship because God's existence encompasses all time ("who was and is and is to come"; Rev 4:8), God has "created all things," and by God's will "they existed and were created" (4:11). God is worthy of worship because only to God do holiness, honor, glory, and power belong. The repetition of the word *holy* three times is known in Jewish literature, and may have its roots in the vision of God in Isaiah 6, where the prophet comes to recognize that God's holiness signifies the belief that God's sovereignty extends over all the world and that, unlike King Uzziah, who died, God's sovereignty is not limited by time or space. God here is described as a God "who lives forever and ever" (Rev 4:10; 5:14; 10:6; 15:7; see also Isa 57:15). As in the vision of Isaiah, here, too, the God who is worshipped is enthroned (4:9). The songs that are offered here in worship emphasize God's transcendence as they announce that holiness, glory, honor, and power belong to God (see also Ps 29:1–2; Rev 11:17–18). But at the same time, the doxology centered on God also proclaims that God willed to create the world and, by God's grace, also sustains the world. God's transcendence above history and culture and God's sustaining love for God's creation provide a significant foundation for building an intercultural worshipping community, because in this way, God cannot be fully known by one culture or through one style of worship. This transcendent God, the creator and sustainer of all, is available to all, relating to them through their historical conditions.

The Nature of God's Centrality in Worship

The next scene in the visions of the throne of God reveals the nature of God's power and enthronement. Two aspects of the nature of God's power are evident. First is the means by which God exercises God's power: through sacrificial love. Second, God shares power with the slaughtered Lamb.

Worship that centers on God is not triumphal, and it is not a place for domination. Worship that centers on God should be marked by shared power and self-giving love for the sake of the other. The seer in Revelation 5:2–5 reports that there was a scroll on the right hand of the enthroned God (5:1). While the seer was weeping because no one was found worthy to open the scroll, one of the elders told him, "Do not weep. See, the Lion of the tribe of Judah, the Root of David, has conquered, so that he can open the scroll and its seven seals" (5:5). Interestingly, this victorious Lion appears as a standing slaughtered Lamb. Indeed, Loren Johns posits that the introduction of Jesus in this way not only highlights "*who* has the keys to history" but also clarifies that "in the switch from lion to lamb is the answer to the unspoken question of *how* he gained that victory."[6] Steven Friesen writes,

> John synthesized in Jesus such images as the Davidic ruler, Servant of the Lord, and the sacrificial Lamb, but he refused to homogenize them. Instead, we are left with startling, unresolved juxtapositions: a lion who appears as a lamb, a slaughtered lamb that lives, a victor who is vanquished. . . . Strength and authority belong not to the one who has practiced violence but rather to the one upon whom violence has been inflicted.[7]

Jesus, the slaughtered Lamb, has conquered not through violence against others but through his faithfulness and sacrificial love. In light of this reversal, the nature of God's power is revealed as the kind of power that is self-giving. Reddish explains,

John's depiction of Christ as a slaughtered lamb with seven horns and seven eyes combines images of death and defeat with symbols of power and authority. Through this imagery John declares that the only "conquering" that is consistent with the values of God is conquering that occurs through self-sacrifice and love, not through violence.[8]

Combining power and self-giving brings to the fore a significant dialectic for envisioning an intercultural church. The members who constitute an intercultural church will have had different experiences in life in relation to suffering and in relation to power. The image of a powerful slaughtered Lamb empowers those who have suffered from violence, rejection, subjugation, and trauma. It also reminds those who hold privilege and power to offer what they have for the sake of others.

The relationship between God and the Lamb in the hymns is also instructive for how the church should think about power. The declarations "You are worthy (*axios*) to take the scroll and to open its seals" (5:9) and "Worthy (*axios*) is the Lamb that was slaughtered to receive power and wealth and wisdom and might and honor and glory and blessing!" (5:12) connect this scene with the preceding worship scene, where the worshippers proclaimed, "You are worthy (*axios*), our Lord" (4:11; see also 1 Chr 29:11). The relation between God and the Lamb is an example of shared power and worthiness (Rev 5:12; Matt 28:18). This is evident in how the hymn of the heavenly beings praises God and the Lamb, making them the center of the worship and adoration by all creation. The vision concludes with these powerful words:

> Then I heard every creature in heaven and on earth and under the earth and in the sea, and all that is in them, singing,
>
> "To the one seated on the throne and to the Lamb be blessing and honor and glory and might forever and ever!"
>
> And the four living creatures said, "Amen!" And the elders fell down and worshiped. (Rev 5:13–14)

What is notable here is there is no competition between God and the Lamb. Power, glory, and honor are shared.

As the church joins in worship with the rest of the creation, the church should be formed by the nature of the relationship between God and the Lamb. Since the church proclaims that glory and might are shared between God and the Lamb, the church is called to learn how to embody its theology not only by worshipping God but also through the relationships between its members. The relation between God and the Lamb is formative for the nature of the worship of the church. John D. Zizioulas argues, "If the church wants to be faithful to her true self, she must try to mirror the communion and otherness that exist in the triune God."[9] The church's belief and worship of the triune God, therefore, calls the church to embrace unity and diversity as a way of being that mirrors how communion and otherness are manifest in the triune God. Zizioulas then adds,

> Communion with the other requires the experience of the *Cross*. . . . Since the Son of God moved to meet the other, his creation, by emptying himself through the

kenosis of the Incarnation, the "kenotic" way is the only one that befits the Christian in his or her communion with the other—be it God or one's neighbor.[10]

Kenosis, which refers to the way Jesus emptied himself (see Phil 2:7), takes on a formative force in the life of the church as it seeks to embody God's love in the world. Intercultural churches can offer a genuine embodiment of a worshipping community whose members seek communion with others who come from different cultural, ethnic, and racial backgrounds. Communion that embraces difference and otherness and that seeks unity is possible through the work of the Spirit, who empowers the church to follow the example of the self-giving of Jesus.

Diversity and Unity

The visions reported in Revelation 5 and 7 reveal the eschatological character of the people of God who offer worship to God and the Lamb. These visions assert that the very nature of the church is a redeemed community that celebrates diversity within unity. In the context of Revelation, if the act of worship is a form of resistance to the empire because worshippers give allegiance only to God, the church as a community that embraces diversity within unity resists cultures of domination or assimilation on the one hand and cultures of segregation or fragmentation on the other hand. As Reddish explains, "Worship is so important in the book of Revelation because John rightly understood that worship is a political act. Through worship one declares one's allegiance, one's loyalty."[11] Worship that is centered on God calls us to resist the temptation to put ourselves and our cultures at the center, and it calls us to repent of trying to impose our own cultures on others. Although diverse worshipping cultures are to be integrated and celebrated in worship, and although worship will always need cultural venues through which to be expressed, the center of worship is, after all, God and not a particular culture. We refocus our worship and ministry on building a community in which difference is seen not as a threat but rather as a blessing that adds to the beauty and strength and richness of the fabric of the community of God.

Because the Lamb is able to open the scroll, the twenty-four elders prostrate themselves before him with harps and golden bowls of incense, singing hymns and praises. They proclaim that Jesus is worthy of worship because through his blood, he has "ransomed for God saints from every tribe and language and people and nation" (Rev 5:9).

Elisabeth Schüssler Fiorenza has shown that the language of ransom or purchase finds its roots in the Greco-Roman context, in which prisoners of war were purchased in order to be brought home, as well as in Exodus, which describes the people of Israel being liberated from Egypt by the blood of the Passover lamb.[12] John uses the language of purchase metaphorically. In light of this, the renewed worshipping community, which is liberated by the work of the Lamb, is called to express its new identity in concrete ways that reflect God's vision for the world, a world in which reconciliation and freedom overcome divisions and bondage.

The song goes on to assert that Jesus has "made them to be a kingdom of priests serving our God, and they will reign on earth" (5:10). In the Hebrew Bible, God called the people of Israel out of slavery so that they would become a worshipping community: "Indeed, the whole earth is mine, but you shall be for me a priestly kingdom and a holy nation" (Exod 19:5–6). In these verses, God asserts God's sovereignty over all of the earth, but God also emphasizes the special relationship between God and the people of Israel—namely, that they have access to God through the office of priesthood and also that they function as priests before God on behalf of all of the earth. According to the hymn of the saints in Revelation 5:9, the circle is expanded to include many people from different languages, tribes, peoples, and nations. Friesen explains, "The saints were priests in the sense that they enjoyed the unmediated presence of the deity, they extended the redemptive work of the Messiah to the rest of the world, and they offered true worship to God."[13] The unity of the worshippers is expressed through their new identity as the ones whom the Lamb ransomed for God; they were made saints and a kingdom of priests. Their unity, however, does not erase their unique identities. In their worship of the Lamb, they acknowledge that their diversity—language, ethnicity, people-hood, or tribal affiliations—can still be recognized.[14]

The cluster of social, political, or cultural affiliations—tribe, language, people, and nation (5:9; 7:9)—recalls the table of the nations in Genesis 10:5, 20, 31, where there is a reference to families, languages, lands, and nations. This language of the diversity of the people of the kingdom of God in Revelation follows the pattern found in the book of Daniel. For example, Daniel 7:14 refers to this diversity in order to underline the universality of the authority of the Mortal One (see Dan 3:4; 5:19; 6:25). The reference to people from every tribe, tongue, people, and nation in Revelation 5:9 also emphasizes "universality."[15] The universality of the church does not refer to assimilating its members under one political, social, or cultural entity. David Aune notes, "Christians were drawn from many ethnic groups in the Roman empire but did not (unlike most Hellenistic religions) constitute an ethnic group themselves."[16] There is continuity between the identity of these people before and after their faith in Jesus. But something new is also emerging for all of them. Followers of Jesus who joined in the chorus of worship do not lose their unique identities. That is, in the kingdom of God, difference is not obliterated. Rather, it adds to the beauty of the people redeemed and called to be God's own. Difference here is not a reason for marginalization or a cause for oppression. All these people have become part of God's people not because they possess more power than others and not because they are a better race than others. They have become God's people despite their differences because they were all redeemed by the blood of the Lamb. And despite the linguistic, cultural, ethnic, and political differences, they have one vocation—namely, becoming a kingdom and priests serving one God.

Differences among the people of God do not lead to segregation in which people are unable to worship or serve together because of their cultural differences, nor does difference cause fragmentation, where all the various groups of the people of God avoid reaching out to the rest of the people of God in order to preserve their own identity. There is diversity but also unity and equality; they are made kings and priests and will reign over the earth. The powerless will be empowered by the new identity they have in Christ (see Rev 22:5; Dan 7:18, 27; Matt 19:28; Rom 5:17). There is no hierarchy in this church because all people, despite their differences, are given a new status through the grace of God. The diversity of the church is held together by the unity of its belief in the work of the Lamb.

Worship and Difference

One of the central challenges that an intercultural church faces has to do with the relation between worship and culture. Some congregations tend to treat their worship style or tradition as a locked treasure chest that can be threatened if opened for modifications to accommodate changes in the demographics of the church. Other congregations act as if they do not have a tradition or a worship style, so they lose opportunities to contribute to the plethora of worship traditions of the church.

> Some congregations tend to treat their worship style or tradition as a closed treasure.

If we assert that worship is the church's mission, then it should be marked by unity that embraces cultural, linguistic, and social diversities, and the church needs to reflect on the relationship between worship and culture.[17] In January 1996, the third international consultation of the Lutheran World Federation's Study Team on Worship and Culture released a statement that has become to be known as the Nairobi State-ment on Worship and Culture.[18] According to this statement, the relationship between worship and culture is multifaceted. Worship is seen as transcultural—that is, there are beliefs (the triune God and the death and resurrection of Jesus) and prac-tices (gathering around the word, baptism, and the Eucharist) that go beyond any given culture. Yet because incarnation is such a central belief in the Christian confession, the contextual-ization of worship in the different cultural settings of the wor-shipping community is an essential aspect of Christian worship. In addition to being transcultural and contextual, worship, according to the Nairobi Statement, is also countercultural and cross-cultural. Worship is countercultural because the gospel of Jesus Christ critiques and transforms cultural practices that are oppressive and sinful. Finally, the statement encourages churches from particular cultures to adopt and adapt elements from other cultures in their worship.

In her reflections on the Nairobi Statement, Anne Zaki describes a crisis that results from mismanaging the relation between worship and culture. The crisis is a coin with two sides. One side focuses on idealizing one's liturgical culture to the point of not being able to change or respond to new needs in one's faith journey, while the other side of the coin is los-ing one's worship tradition by assimilating into another domi-nant culture. According to Zaki, there are some Christians who "try to blend in by matching their beliefs and practices—their entire religion, form, and foundation—to those of the con-temporary culture."[19] She adds that other Christians solve the tension between their faith and culture by "isolating themselves in opposition to the culture." She explains, "This can take the passive shape of retreating to fundamentalist convictions, insisting that faith must be practiced in its original and purest forms, crediting the 'good ole days' for bygone exuberance and growth. But it can also become aggressive, imposing itself on others, fighting about differences in worldview, faith, and practices."[20] Relying on the Nairobi Statement, Zaki suggests that churches do well to recognize the relation between worship and culture as a dance. In this dance, "each dancer has certain steps to perform, yet always remains conscious of a partner—now pulling together, now pushing apart, ever moving, avoiding the checkmate crises."[21]

In addition to establishing theological understanding for what worship is, the visions of the throne of God in Revelation 4–7 animate important insights about the relation between worship and culture. These insights include diversity in expressions of worship, a healthy relation between innovation and tradition, and intercultural worship creating spaces for genuine expression of faith through spiritualities of lament and praise.

Innovation and Tradition

As I have noted already in this chapter, the hymns of praise and adoration that are proclaimed in order to glorify God and the Lamb show a great deal of continuity between the two parts of the Bible. This continuity shows that the story of God is one story that encompasses the people of Israel and the church.

Among those who offer praises to God and the Lamb are the twenty-four elders. The number twenty-four represents the sum of the twelve tribes of Israel and the twelve disciples of Jesus (see Rev 21:12–14). By bringing the Jewish and the gentile believers together, John not only emphasizes the diversity and the unity of the church but also the continuity and innovation within the worshipping community as part of God's salvific work.

As angelic beings in the presence of God, the elders represent the church. They are a priestly kingdom; therefore, John describes them as wearing golden crowns and offering incense before God. The new song signifies that the work of God in Jesus is a turning point in history. The metaphor of ransoming saints is an economic one that speaks of purchasing the freedom of those who were enslaved; in other words, the work of salvation in Christ is an act of liberation. This reminds us of the exodus from Egypt, where the Israelites were redeemed or ransomed by God from their slavery to Pharaoh to become worshippers or servants of God. And in a similar way, as God ransomed the people of Israel from bondage, Jesus ransoms saints for God. In both cases, those who were ransomed have a new destiny and a new identity as "a kingdom of priests" (Rev 5:9–10; Exod 19:6). As important as it is to emphasize continuity in God's story, it is also important to highlight the point that something significantly new has emerged in God's salvation in Jesus Christ. The newness of the work of the Lamb, therefore, is reflected in the way the text describes the worship that is offered to the Lamb as a "new song" (Rev 5:9).

The phrase "new song" (*shir chadash*) occurs also in the Hebrew Bible. Aune notes that the expression "refers to the introduction of a new composition for the purpose of celebrating a very special occasion, or the introduction of a new composition into a setting in which many songs have been used traditionally for a very long time."[22] The "new song" in these passages in the Old Testament celebrates the divine salvation of God's people as well as an invitation for the nations to recognize the saving work of God. Although some of these texts speak of the particularity of the relationship between God and God's people, they also open a space for outsiders to join the chorus of praise. The phrase occurs where the people of God are called to praise God using different instruments and to utter words that describe God's justice and faithfulness in sustaining the creation and in redeeming the oppressed (Pss 33:3; 40:3; 144:9; 149:1; Isa 42:10). Offering a new song proclaims God's just and upright reign over all the nations; the peoples and the nations are exhorted to present worship before God in words of praise, offerings, and prostration (96:1; 98:1). A "new song," then, could refer to playing new instruments in worship, composing new words to praise God for rescuing a people from different forms of oppression, and calling out to new peoples and nations to celebrate the just and upright reign of God.

The new song that reflects God's act of widening the circle to include many believers from different cultures, nations, peoples, and languages calls for multiple ways of offering worship to God. Carol Doran and Thomas H. Troeger frame tradition and renewal in worship using the metaphor of a tribe. They offer an intriguing discussion of "the benefits and limitations of belonging to a tribe," on the one hand, and "the benefits and limitations of pluralism and popular culture." They emphasize the importance of understanding and appreciating the history of a particular congregation's worship in order to be able to introduce changes in a meaningful and healthy way. Understanding people's "memories and the highest hopes of their hearts" helps them see that the renewal in worship is not meant "*to take away from* their worship, but to expand and deepen their sense of the living God."[23]

Innovation and renewal in worship, and moving toward pluralistic expressions of worship or envisioning intercultural worship, will always have to engage people's cultures. Doran and Troeger argue that "a balanced critical perspective on the liabilities and benefits of our culture is a necessary prerequisite for revitalizing worship in our own age."[24] They assert that the gospel "was presented in a manner that could engage people's imagination, and that would not have been possible without establishing some critical connections with the culture. The worship of the communities that gave us the Bible was vitalized by a critical relationship to culture, neither completely rejecting nor completely accepting its forms of expression."[25]

Word and Body

In a careful reading of the visions of Revelation 4–7, one notices that alongside worship of God and the Lamb using words, there are bodily and symbolic acts of worshipping God. The expressions "falling down" (*piptein*) and "worshipping" (*proskunein*) are paired again in the book of Revelation (cf. 5:14; 7:11; 11:16; 19:10; 22:8). One of the key words that John uses for worship entails a bodily posture—namely, bowing down (*proskuneō*). This verb refers to the recognition of God's sovereignty, so worship in the bodily form of prostrating oneself intends to show that only God the creator, redeemer, and sustainer is worthy of worship. According to Friesen, "For John, one crucial aspect of worship was allegiance. Bowing down was a physical enactment of submission to divine authority."[26] Bowing down and prostrating are bodily gestures that reflect recognition of who God is. Here we find worship that is holistic in that it includes proclamation by words and also by embodied expression of adoration.

The proclaimed words and the embodied adoration are also accompanied by a symbolic action that animates the point that only God is the center of the act of worship. The twenty-four elders "cast their crowns before the throne" (Rev 4:10). In some parts of the Bible, crowns were taken off a defeated king (2 Sam 1:10; 12:30). In the context of Revelation, however, taking off the crowns and placing them before the throne is a voluntary act performed by the twenty-four elders. Such an action intends to show submission and recognition that the ultimate power lies with God. This posture can be challenging and troubling. Those who want to hold onto their privileges—their crowns—are challenged to give up their sense of security or exceptionalism. In worship, humans are called to face their fears by putting their trust in God and not in the idols of pseudo-supremacy they have created for themselves. This posture can be troubling for those who are already pressed or deprived or who have had their honor and power snatched away because of political, economic, or cultural ideologies that marginalize them. It is important to note here that the text of Revelation was written to give hope to the marginalized church. For John, worshipping God through words and body generates hope for the oppressed because God is a just God who is capable of defending and protecting them (7:14–17).

In addition to words and bodily postures, the worship in the visions also includes playing music and burning incense that represents the prayers of the saints (Rev 5:8). Mitchell Reddish offers this commentary about the scene:

> The elders participate continually in the worship and praise of God, prostrating themselves, offering prayers and incense, and play their harps to provide music for the heavenly liturgy. They are heavenly examples of the pure worship of God, models for the churches on earth to follow. They serve also as a contrast to the worship that is occurring elsewhere on earth, the worship of the emperor. The only one truly deserving of worship is the one who sits enthroned in the heavens.[27]

What is noticeable here is that worship engages the mental capacities of the worshipping community as they utter meaningful words of worship that express and articulate their belief in God. At the same time, the worship is holistic in that it integrates the body that bows down, the hands that play the instruments, and the noses that smell the sweet aroma of the incense.

Worship in an intercultural church should embrace the diverse ways through which people express their allegiance to God. Worship in such a setting will entail a growing edge and a learning curve and some uncomfortable articulations of worship. When people who come from different cultural backgrounds worship together, there will have to be a space for familiarity and for estrangement. Being uncomfortable in worship might be intimidating for many people, but this experience of discomfort can also create a space for the work of the Spirit to draw the church deeper into the mystery of God. Kathy Black says it this way:

> When people who come from different cultural backgrounds worship together, there will have to be a space for familiarity and for estrangement.

> If nothing is unsettling, if nothing forces us out of the familiar, if there is no room for the unexpected, then there is also no room for mystery and therefore no room for God or the Holy Spirit to work in our lives. Change is unsettling; letting go is often unsettling. But it is often in these experiences that we make room for the Divine to enter our lives.[28]

For this "unsettling" to happen in healthy and constructive ways, a congregation needs to understand its tradition, and it also needs to open itself up for worship styles to be integrated so that the different groups feel they are part of the church and not an add-on. Kathy Black suggests that worship planners should be able to identify what is comforting and what is unsettling for those who are involved in worship "so that the design, content, and style of worship can provide a balance whereby both the comforting and the unsettling is [*sic*] present for *all*."[29]

Praise and Lament

In the previous sections, I have outlined the centrality of the language of praise, hymn, and doxology in explaining why God and the Lamb are worthy of worship. The visions that are reported in Revelation 4–7 begin with doxologies of adoration (Revelation 4–5) and end with hymns of praise (Revelation 7). But in the middle (Revelation 6), the reader is confronted with the troubling reality of pain and suffering. This way, the book of Revelation creates an important space for lament and protest in the midst of praise. Because people come from different backgrounds, an intercultural church should create space for people to express their experiences of trauma and losses.

Apocalyptic literature, such as Revelation, offers two simultaneous scenes: one is of the glory, power, and harmony of the divine throne, while the other is the chaos, death, and destruction that the created world is experiencing. The beauty and majesty of the scene by the throne inspire praise, while the reality of persecution and oppression calls for lament and protest. As the scene shifts from the awesomeness of the divine throne, where the songs of praise circulate in an endless chorus glorifying God and the Lamb, John is called to "see" the mysteries of the seven seals. These seals, along with the other sevenfold series (trumpets and bowls), speak of disasters that will blow across the earth (Revelation 6; 8–9; 15–16). These three sevenfold series should not be interpreted as predicting future world events; rather, they use different symbols, a prominent feature of apocalyptic literature, to depict the calamites and the chaos that is taking place on earth and to create a space in the midst of persecution for the faithful ones to find hope.

The first sevenfold series uses the symbol of seals to reveal the reality that the world undergoes (Rev 6:1–17; 8:1–4). Unlike the first four seals, which speak of death and destruction on earth, the fifth seal speaks of the martyrs, whose souls are under an altar in heaven (Rev 6:9–11). These martyrs who have sacrificed their lives for testifying to the gospel are now calling upon God: "Sovereign Lord, holy and true, how long will it be before you judge and avenge our blood on the inhabitants of the earth?" (6:10). The location of these saints, under the altar, and the words they utter urge God to manifest God's vindication for the oppressed and justice upon the oppressor.[30] For the most part, worship in churches does not leave room for outcries like the one we see here in the book of Revelation. Worship, according to Revelation 4–7, should create a space for human anguish as well as human thanksgiving. Reddish summarizes this way:

> Worship is devalued also when it is not allowed to give voice to the full range of human feelings toward God. Granted, worship is primarily praise, thanksgiving, and adoration. Those themes should dominate both our private and corporate worship of God. But there are

times when cries of anguish, despair, and even doubt are appropriate in worship. In Revelation 6:9–11, the souls of the martyrs under the heavenly altar cry out in agony to God, "How long?" Such cries have a rightful place in worship. . . . A faithful worshipping community is able to gather all its experiences and troubles and offer them up to God, confident that God will hear their cries of pain as readily as God will hear their hymns of praise.[31]

Comparing the prayer of the martyrs with the traditions of the Hebrew Bible, one realizes that this prayer combines two types of psalms—psalms of lament and psalms of revenge, or imprecatory psalms. One common aspect of these two types of psalms is that they create a space in worship in which the powerless and the oppressed ones become agents of change through prayer, and thus they regain some of the power that the oppressors sought to deprive them of. In these two types of psalms, the psalmists exercise their faith in God by expressing both their complaint and their protests. In other words, as the psalmists offer their worship to God, they do not cover up for the mess and chaos that surrounds them, and they do not gloss over the pain and suffering that they have endured. As these psalmists take their prayers to God, they emphasize not only their trust in God but also that they choose not to exercise violence against those who persecute them. They take responsibility to act by naming the violence and by reminding God of God's covenant. Even so, they wait upon God to act and to bring about justice. They are not passively waiting for God; they continue to live faithfully and righteously.

Human complaint and protests are not directed solely to God; as a matter of fact, psalms of revenge name the violence that is done by the wicked against the righteous and faithful (Psalm 109). Furthermore, in many of the psalms of lament and protest, the psalmists name human enemies, some of whom are even companions in the sanctuary (Psalm 55). In other words, worship is not just about being happy and jubilant. It is also about responding honestly to reality without losing sight of hope in God. Whether worship involves praise or lament, thanksgiving or protest, it creates a space for church members to be real and speak truthfully in God's presence.

In an intercultural church in which people come together from different walks of life, worship should reflect people's diverse experiences. Making room for diversity in worship is not a way of covering up divisions, hatred, and racism. Praising God makes the church realize that the mountains of racism and the long history of segregation and stigma and oppression can be moved by the power of God. But at the same time, when believers lament and protest, they articulate

> When the church creates a space for lament and protest, it cultivates a ground for honesty.

their frustration, disappointment, and pain, and they call out to God to deliver them from the injustices they experience. When the church creates a space for lament and protest, it cultivates the ground for honesty between Christians as they talk to God and one another about hurt, pain, and divisions.

In this way, intercultural worship is not just worship that uses different songs from different countries or employs different languages; rather, it is worship that creates a space for people to speak honestly about their experience of God and the other. Kathleen O'Connor explains, "The point of lament is not to confess sin, though such confession deserves an honored place in liturgy, but to name injustice, hurt, and anger. Prayers of lament are not about what is wrong *with us* but about wrong done *to us*."[32]

Many Christians are uncomfortable with the language of lament and protest. Some think lament and protest are signs of lack of faith in God. The language of protest in the psalms is quite strong in its way of questioning God's justice in the midst of painful realities (see, e.g., Psalms 44 and 74). Even so, some Christians try to soften the words of lament and consider these texts to be mere expressions of anger, or they dismiss the psalms as only human words that should not be taken as seriously as the psalm texts that offer the language of trust and praise. Besides making theological assumptions that marginalize the language of lament in the church, people respond to the language of lament or protest quite often according to their social and political experiences. Sometimes people's experiences with freedom of speech in political and social circles affect the way they relate to an authority figure like God.

Whether the reasons are theological or social, communal and individual worship and faith journeys suffer tremendous loss because of the marginalization of the language of lament. Walter Brueggemann underscores the consequences of losing sight of lament as a form of faithful discourse in engaging

God and the world.[33] He says that one of the key losses is that we ignore an essential way of becoming covenantal partners with God, because when we lament and protest, we urge God to do justice in the world. The loss of the language of lament threatens the covenantal relation because one party becomes voiceless or is permitted only one voice—that of praise. Derek Suderman rightly points out that Brueggemann's treatment of lament focuses only on God and the petitioner. Suderman seeks to underline the importance of a third party that is essential to lament—a listening community that is dedicated to hearing the cries and discerning a faithful response. When lament is lost, the church loses its commitment and ability to listen, to empathize, and even respond to the injustice experienced by other parts of the body of Christ or our neighbors outside the church.[34]

Intercultural churches that create space for lament in worship will deepen Christian formation and generate new hope in God, who is true and just. Facing the reality of lament also empowers the faith community to become agents of change. As William Blaine-Wallace writes,

> I believe the principal task of the church in present-day [North] America is to reclaim and restore our Judeo-Christian pathos, a tradition of grieving that both encourages and equips us to embrace our present experiences of suffering and death toward freeing engagement in and for a world groaning in travail.

Blaine-Wallace explains that Watts Street Baptist Church in North Carolina practices solidarity in worship by opening services with psalms of lament, which they call "the public processing of pain":

> They take their processed pain to the streets, holding prayer vigils at the site of each violent death in Durham. Public grief offers more than the road to freedom for the oppressed. Public grief creates the strongest possibility for more genuine reconciliation between the perpetrators of violence, tyranny, power abusers, and their victims. . . . Reconciliation worth its salt begins with the victims' public expression of grief and, if at all possible, in the presence of their perpetrators.[35]

Because the task of healing the wounds and restoring peace and justice in the world is bigger than the human agents, the language of lament expresses the church's trust in God and in God's salvific power. Worship affirms that despair is not the last word. The creator God is also active in saving the world that God loves through the costly work of Jesus Christ the slain Lamb.

In the vision that is recorded in Revelation 7, after hearing the saints express their anguish before God, the seer reports that he saw in heaven a great multitude that no one could count. This crowd came from "every nation, from all tribes and peoples and languages" (Rev 7:9). Reddish observes that "this innumerable crowd is inclusive, encompassing people from every racial, ethnic, political, and linguistic background."[36] What brought this crowd together in worship, despite their apparent differences, was that they were ransomed and purified through the blood of the Lamb (7:14; see also Lev 17:11). This crowd was dressed in white robes and was holding palm branches, both signs of victory (1 Macc 13:51; John 12:13). The throng of the redeemed ones offers a song of praise before God in adoration of the God who saved them from the tribulation. The prayers of complaint offered from under the altar of God are transformed. Their prayers have been heard. In worship before God, they sing, "Salvation belongs to our God who is seated on the throne, and to the Lamb!" (7:10).

The singers recognize that it is God and the Lamb who have worked to save and deliver them from death and disasters. Those who have resisted the empire lead all of those who are present before God in jubilation and thanksgiving. Because they have trusted in the victory of the Lamb despite the persecution they had to endure, they now stand before the throne of God. They are honored to be servants who minister in God's temple day and night, and in their midst God dwells. They will not get hungry or thirsty, and they will not be harmed by the sun because the Lamb will shepherd them and guide them to springs of living water.

When people gather to worship in an intercultural church, they bring with them different experiences of pain and shame. Some are in pain because they are suffering from cultures of misogyny, racism, and violence; others are ashamed because they have abused power at the expense of others or have been complacent about cultures of segregation or domination. Some Christians experience hopelessness even in the midst of worship; they have no place in worship to express their pains, their apathy, or their doubt that things can change. An intercultural church that brings people from different ethnicities, races, languages, and cultures to worship together can offer the world a sign of hope. They can show how God is at work to bring people who are different from one another to worship God and serve one another. Worship is an expression of trust in God in both praise or in lament; such genuine worship is capable of generating hope that God is transforming the world.

Discussion Questions

1. In what way is God's mission in the world connected to or driven by worship? How are worshipping communities "signs" of God's activity in this world?
2. How can the vision in Revelation 4–7 inform an understanding of what it means to be an intercultural church?
3. On each of the following continuums, mark how would you characterize the worship provided by your faith community:

   a. _____

   closed   open

   b. _____

   monocultural   intercultural

   c. _____

   oriented inward   oriented outward

4. Talk together about your perceptions. How might you like to see your perceptions change?

5. What would worship in an intercultural church look like? Who would plan it? Have you ever experienced intercultural worship? If so, describe the experience.

6. Why is attention to lament so important in building intercultural worship models?

4

Babel and Pentecost: Moving from Being Monocultural to Being Intercultural

Building an intercultural church or society requires its individuals to communicate with one another. The most obvious challenge to achieving desired communication arises when the members of the church or the community do not know one another's languages. People are in contact with and in relation with others at places of employment, neighborhoods, churches, parks, or other public places where they do not share the same language. Some individuals learn new languages in order to be able to communicate with other members of the society or the church, but others take a hard-line posture, including the demand that everyone speak the language of the dominant group. Two recent books open with practical questions that underline the tension around language, identity, and integration:

Why don't they all just speak English?[1]
Why are you forcing me to sing in other languages?[2]

These questions highlight the tension around the role of language in the process of forming an intercultural community or a church.

This chapter will engage these questions by looking into the narratives of the Tower of Babel and Pentecost. These two narratives will be addressed with special attention to the issue of linguistic diversity. Is diversity of languages and cultures part of the divine plan for human communities? Or is it a sign of judgment, punishment, and alienation? How do Babel and Pentecost relate to each other? Does Pentecost undo Babel; that is, is Pentecost a reversal of Babel? Or is Pentecost a continuation of Babel? Put differently, is there something gained at Babel that Pentecost maintains, yet is there something lost at Babel that Pentecost restores or resolves?

This discussion will suggest that, according to one reading of the narrative of Babel, God's vision for human communities is to move from being monocultural to becoming multicultural and multilinguistic communities. Yet as the first chapter explained, being a multicultural or multilinguistic church or community is not the end goal. Although multiculturalism is a great step toward accepting cultural and linguistic difference, the concern is that people will end up forming islands within the same community while avoiding deep engagement with one another. A multicultural community needs to create a space in which the people can interact with one another, get to know each other, and be transformed together; a multilinguistic community needs the gift of translation so that communication and knowledge can be possible. Therefore, it is important to highlight that Pentecost and the gift of languages given by the Spirit enable the church to become intercultural, that is, a community in which communication and interaction are possible not because one language dominates but rather because of the ability to speak each other's languages. Thus, Pentecost embraces diversity but creates a space where those who are different are able to communicate.

Language and Identity

Before digging deeper into the Babel and Pentecost narratives, it is appropriate to highlight the significance of language for communal identity. Readers of the Bible may be familiar with one of the key issues that the returnees from the exile wrestled with—namely, the marriage of Judean men to foreign women. Both Ezra and Nehemiah followed a hard-line purity politics that treated marriage to foreign wives as a threat to the identity of the whole people and, therefore, mistreated these women by having the Judean men divorce them. It should be noted that texts such as the book of Ruth and Isaiah 56, which speak of the inclusion of the foreign and the religious other in the people of God, offer an alternative to Ezra and Nehemiah's exclusionary politics. The postexilic community did not just struggle with the issues around intermarriage. Language also was part of the community's struggles.

Nehemiah reports that many Jews married women from Ashdod, Ammon, and Moab. He goes on to mentions that "half of their children spoke the language of Ashdod, and they could not speak the language of Judah, but spoke the language of various peoples" (Neh 13:24). Because this verse does not provide a lot of details, many questions remain unanswered. For instance, why does the text single out the language of Ashdod? Is it because it is a non-Semitic language, so it refers to maximum foreignness in this context? Why does the text say only half the children were unable to speak the language of Judah? Did some parents do a better job of teaching their kids Hebrew than others, who were not able to teach their kids their home language? Or were the children of different ages, and their linguistic abilities depended on how much they had interacted with people who spoke one language and not the other? Although we cannot answer all these questions with certainty, we can acknowledge that language was one of the identity questions facing the community of Persian Judah.

It seems clear that Nehemiah was disturbed by the fact that half the children were unable to speak the language of Judah. Nehemiah quarreled with those Jews, and he even used violence against them, including beating them and pulling out their hair (13:25). It is unclear whether he did this because they had married foreign women, failed to teach their children Hebrew, or both. At any rate, it seems from this incident that language was central to the identity of the community, and Nehemiah was either disappointed that the second generation did not speak Hebrew or angry because the children spoke only one language, a foreign one. It is interesting to note that, eventually, the Hebrew Bible was translated into Aramaic and Greek in order to accommodate the needs of the Jewish diaspora.

The situation that Nehemiah struggled with is well known among migrant communities that struggle with the issue of language in varieties of ways. Some immigrants are unable to learn a new language because they have migrated as older adults; other migrants struggle to teach their children their home language and feel disappointed that their children cannot communicate with them in their mother tongue. This phenomenon is also experienced in the church, where many congregations that host migrant communities cannot integrate newcomers because of linguistic barriers. Some congregations use translation devices, and others sing songs in different languages. Some congregations seek to maintain a monolingual setting by asking individuals to assimilate into the language of the dominant group. Other

> Many congregations that host migrant communities cannot integrate newcomers because of linguistic barriers.

ethnic congregations do not accommodate the second generation, continuing to worship in the original language of the parent generation. An intercultural church that embraces a multilingual approach to worship, fellowship, and ministry not only could be a place where diverse communities are welcomed but also a place that responds pastorally to migrant families who are anxious about the future of their traditions, languages, and cultures. In this interlinguistic community, individuals are encouraged to learn each other's language and therefore are invited to understand each other's cultures and worldviews, which are not only expressed by language but also constituted, in part, by it.

The Tower of Babel

The narrative of the Tower of Babel in Genesis 11 begins with this intriguing statement: "Now the whole earth had one language and the same words" (11:1). Having one language and the same words makes communication possible, but it also underscores sameness and similarity. Having one language limits the scope of cultural innovation. In Genesis 11, the human community migrates or rather "sets out" (*ns'*) from the east to the plains of Shinar, where they settle. Given that they have the same language, they are able to communicate and invent something new: making bricks and using bitumen for mortar. That they had similar words is evident in the way the Hebrew text of verse 3 describes their first invention; the English translation does not allow the reader to appreciate the repetition of consonants. Reproducing it in transliterated Hebrew with a literal translation in English might help the reader to notice the limitations of the scope of their language:

Wayomero ish el re'ehu (They said each one to his mate) *haba nilebena lebenim wenisrepha(h) lisrepha(h)*

("Come, let us brick bricks, and burn burning") *watehi lahem hallbena(h) le'aben wehakhemar haya(h) lahem lakhomer* (and they had brick for stone, and bitumen for mortar).

Developing the ability to make bricks and use bitumen inspires them to build for themselves "a city and a tower with its top in the heavens" (11:4).

Building the city and the tower serves them in two ways: it makes a name for them, and it protects them from being scattered all over the earth (11:4). While the human community seeks to build a tower that reaches the heavens, the Lord comes down to investigate their project (11:5). In the Lord's evaluation of the situation, the Lord emphasizes their sameness: "They are one people, and they all have one language." The Lord then concludes that "nothing they propose to do will now be impossible for them" (11:6).

With the exception of Psalm 17:3 and Zechariah 8:15, the word *zmm*, translated "propose," has negative connotations (see Deut 19:19; Isa 32:7); the root is used to describe God's judgment over the people (Jer 4:28; 30:24), and it is even used to describe the purpose (*zmm*) of the Lord to destroy Babel (Jer 51:11–12). The divine plan diverts the human projects of maintaining sameness and resisting the divine command to fill the earth. God's diversion plan is to make them speak different languages and therefore to make them unable to understand each other's speech. "Come, let us go down, and confuse (*nblh*) their language there, so that they will not understand one another's speech" (11:7). The confusion of languages could mean one of two things: either they continue speaking the same language but lose the ability to "hear" or "understand" (Heb. *shm'*) the words uttered by their friends, or they start speaking different languages, which also results in their inability to communicate as one community, so they are unable to finish their project.

The Lord then scatters them over the face the earth. As a result, the project that was under way because they all spoke one language, which hindered them from being scattered over the earth, stops. God does not destroy the work they accomplished. God brings humanity back to the initial intent of the creation story—to fill the earth (Gen 1:28; 9:1). It should be noted, however, that the word used in Genesis 1 and 9 is *mla'* (to fill), while the word used in Genesis 11:4, 8, 9 is *puts* (to scatter), which is used in some of the prophetic texts to speak of the exile (see, for example, Jer 9:16; Ezek 22:15). The spreading out of humans all over the earth is enforced by the repetition of the word *sham* (there) in 11:2, 7, 8, 9; that is, they sought to settle there, but from there, God sends them away. Further, the word *sham* (there) recalls other sounds that are present in the narrative: *shammayim* (heavens; 11:4) and *shem* (name; 11:4, 9). Humans sought a name for themselves by reaching up to the heavens, and God descends from the heavens to see their project, to which God has given a name: Babel (Heb. *babel*), because there God confuses (Heb. *bll*) the speech of all the earth. The narrative is ambiguous enough to allow for various interpretations, and none of them is definitive.

Divine Judgment of Human Sin

The first approach to the story of the Tower of Babel reads the narrative as yet another incident of human sin and divine judgment. According to this approach, humans in this narrative continue what Adam and Eve did in the garden of Eden—namely, seeking independence from God. In this view, phrases like "a tower with its top in the heavens" and "let us make a name for ourselves" indicate human pride. Human arrogance leads the people to believe they can make themselves immortal. A classic example of understanding the story of the tower as a manifestation of human pride can be found in Saint Augustine's sermons on the Gospel of John:

> For once the tongues became discordant through pride, and then of one became many tongues. For after the flood certain proud men, as if endeavoring to fortify themselves against God, as if anything were high for God, or anything could give security to pride, raised a tower, apparently that they might not be destroyed by a flood, should there come one thereafter. For they had heard and considered that all iniquity was swept away by a flood; to abstain from iniquity they would not; they sought the height of a tower as a defense against a flood; they built a lofty tower.[3]

According to this interpretation, multiplicity of language is a result of human pride. The issue with this reading of the story is that it imposes categories such as pride or arrogance on mundane expressions of human aspiration. Building a tower with its top to the heavens does not necessarily need to be a challenge against God; it could simply refer to a tower that is really tall (cf. Deut 1:28; 9:1). Furthermore, the tower is not the main goal of the human project; they wanted to build a city, a tower, and a name so that they would not be dispersed over all the earth. In addition, the phrase "let us make a name for ourselves" can possibly be referring to creating a unified identity for this human community. Theodore Hiebert understands this phrase to "express no conceit or defiance but rather the impulse toward cultural homogeneity."[4] John Howard Yoder also critiques the reading of the tower of Babel in terms of sin and judgment. He contends that the reader should not

> assume that God is *only* scattering the people as a form of punishment. Nowhere does the text identify it as punishment. It is only punishment if one presumes that monological centralized existence is in the people's best interest. Yet it was God's good intention, as stated in the beginning (Gen 1:28) and reaffirmed after the flood (Gen 9:7), that humans would scatter and fill the earth. This is precisely what the people seeking to make a name for themselves were trying to avoid (Gen 11:4) and what God assured would happen by confusing their speech (Gen 11:7–9).

Human Homogeneity

A second approach to understanding the Tower of Babel story does not put the emphasis on human pride in relation to God, but rather it emphasizes humans' desire for homogeneity. According to this reading, the emphasis does not lie in the tower or the name but rather in the city, which represents oppressive imperial domination. Ched Myers explains this approach: "The ancient folktale of 'Babel' in Genesis 11 best expresses the antipathy of those living in the oppressive shadow of the great city-states." For Myers, "the building of the project there represents the centripetal power of urban empire. Life in Babel is fundamentally characterized by centralization of purpose (the construction of a tower) and cultural conformity (they all spoke one language)."[5]

Cities prosper and survive by controlling human and natural resources, and they protect their success by exercising oppressive military power over all that surrounds the city. Myers explains, "Imperial urban societies sought to domesticate nature, bringing the wild sacred 'into captivity.'"[6] Civilization of the imperial city-states distorted "the proper human relationship to both the divine and the natural," an act that could be thought of as "the human fall from original communion."[7] The real issue in Genesis 11, in this view, is "imperial *monoculture*." While the imperial project is characterized by social, political, and cultural centralization, "the divine antidote to the centripetal, homogenizing project of empire is a redispersion of peoples (11:8), symbolized here by both linguistic/cultural variety and geographic diffusion."[8] Myers goes on to suggest that since dispersal of humans all over the earth was God's original plan (Gen 1:28; 9:1), dispersal of the people in Genesis 11 should not be seen as a judgment from God, "but rather an act of *centrifugal* liberation from urban monoculture and superconcentration."[9]

This interpretation of Genesis 11 celebrates diversity of language and culture as a divine gift and not as a divine judgment. Yet it is interesting to note that this interpretation is similar to the traditional interpretation of Genesis 11, previously described, in that both see the project taking place in Babel in a negative light. The traditional interpretation considers building the tower a rebellion against God, but this second interpretation speaks of human sin in connection to the domination of the empire.

While I agree that centralization seems to be an issue in the text, I think using the language of empire to speak of the people in Babel seems to impose a concept that is not present in the text. Genesis 11 does not speak of conflict between the peoples; as a matter of fact, there seems to be harmony. With no other communities over which they could exercise power, their language is participatory ("let us"), and they always speak in the plural. It is true that they are a monocultural and monolingual community. But I would rather speak of this reality in terms of unity and sameness, not domination and empire. Furthermore, although dispersal does yield diversity, experiences of exile and making people refugees suggest that dispersal could be painful. When we celebrate the multiplicity of languages and cultures, it is important to remember the pain of those who are forced to live in diaspora. Fernandez explains that "diaspora is about the experience of being uprooted, dispersed, displaced, and dislocated as well as the search for roots and connections."[10]

The Origins of Cultural Difference

A third approach reads the story of the Tower of Babel as a narrative that is, in the words of Theodore Hiebert, "exclusively about the origins of cultural difference and not about pride and punishment at all." Hiebert explains, "The story's terminology, explicit claims, and repetitive structure all focus on the tension between singularity and multiplicity with the purpose of explaining the origin and variety of the world's cultures."[11] Thus, the story in Genesis 11 is not primarily about the tower but rather about the fact that at the beginning of the story, humans were speaking one language, and by the end of the narrative, they were speaking multiple languages. This is evident in that both the narrator and God state that the people speak the same language (11:1, 6). Hiebert goes on to assert that although the narrative does explain the origin of the name of the city Babylon, the people who are building the city and the tower are not the Babylonians. Therefore, he rejects identifying these humans with the empire or the city-state of Nimrod, king of Babylon (Gen 10:8–10):

> The storyteller mentions no king with imperial pretensions, but attributes the project in vv. 1–4 to the people, using plural pronouns and verbs throughout. No uniquely royal or imperial language is present. Furthermore, empire is anachronistic within the boundaries of this story, which is about the entire human race, not about one culture imposing its will on another. The single

language that all of the people speak is not imposed by an imperial edict but reflects the reality of a single family surviving the flood. The aim of the project . . . has nothing to do with extending the reach of empire but just the opposite: staying in one place (v. 4). The story, thus, is not about the suppression of difference between cultures but about the origins of difference itself.[12]

In Genesis 11:6, God does not feel threatened by the human adventures; God simply acknowledges that humans have one language and are one people, so God emphasizes their sameness. Further, God acknowledges that they have accomplished part of their aspirations—namely, building a city and a tower. Therefore, it seems likely they will succeed in remaining in one location. God's intervention then is to multiply the languages (11:7, 9)[13] and therefore multiply cultures, since language is one of the primary ways of forming cultural identity. God "mixes" (Heb. *bll*) up their languages, with the result that the people are unable to understand each other—not as a punishment, but as a result of the introduction of many new and distinct languages. Multiplying the languages is followed by dispersing the human race all over the earth.

Genesis 11 uses language and geography, two important markers of cultural identity, to explain how the human race was transformed from a monocultural into a multicultural community. In Hiebert's words, "Geographical residence—a people's land or territory—is closely associated, as is language, with the identity of a specific culture or ethnic group, and it is a prominent means of distinction between cultures. . . . God's two actions, distinguishing languages and dispersing humanity, explain the origin of the world's cultures and provide an etiology of cultural difference."[14]

Hiebert's reading of the narrative of the Tower of Babel moves in a helpful direction in that it celebrates linguistic and cultural diversity. But even such a positive reading of the divine intervention in human affairs leaves out an important aspect— namely, that these humans lost their ability to communicate. And although difference in itself is something to embrace and celebrate, difference without the ability to understand the other language and the other culture may well leave people fragmented, scattered, and possibly afraid of the unknown other. This fear might lead to the use of power to subjugate the ones who are not known to be friends. In other words, before the divine intervention, human sameness in language and culture limited the potential of the creative work of God among the human community, which lacked diversity. But after the divine intervention, the human community enjoyed multiplicity in language and culture. But without the ability to communicate, humans might experience fragmentation or competition.

Blessing and Challenge

In my view, the divine intervention puts an end to a human project. It is interesting to note that God is not condemning building a city or a tower, nor is God condemning the peoples' ambition to make a name for themselves, that is, to be remembered.

The issue here is not what they have done but what they can do or accomplish. Humans want to protect themselves from being scattered all over the earth by centralizing their efforts around a project. They are able to do that because of their sameness—specifically, their ability to speak the same language. When God confuses their lips or their speech so they become unable to understand each other, humans gain the blessing of speaking different languages, but they also lose the ability to communicate. In other words, divine intervention in the human project of sameness brings a blessing and also a challenge. I think the story of the Tower of Babel is about the human community moving from being monolingual and monocultural (urban, sedentary, centralized) to becoming multicultural (urban, nomadic, rural) and multilingual. The question then remains: As humans experience this diversity, is there a way for them to communicate, or will they compete over power and control, with the dominant forcing others to become like them culturally and linguistically.

Pentecost

Pentecost was one of three yearly festivals in which Jews and God-fearing gentiles made a pilgrimage to Jerusalem. After the ascension of Jesus, the disciples went back to Jerusalem with a task and a promise. They were commissioned to witness to God's salvific work in Jerusalem, Judea, Samaria, and the whole earth. And Jesus had promised they would receive the gift of the Spirit, who would empower them to fulfill their ministry (Acts 1:8). When it was the time of Pentecost, while all of them had gathered in one place, the disciples were filled with the Spirit, and they began to speak in other languages according to the gift of the Spirit. The event is described in words that are awe inspiring: "And suddenly from heaven there came a sound like the rush of a violent wind, and it filled the entire house where they were sitting. Divided tongues, as of fire, appeared among them, and a tongue rested on each of them" (2:2–4).

Present in Jerusalem at this time were "devout Jews from every nation under heaven" (2:5). Beverly Gaventa notes that "by the first century, far more Jews lived outside Palestine than within it."[15] Some diaspora Jews would make a pilgrimage to Jerusalem for Passover and Pentecost, and others ended up living again in Jerusalem for the purpose of trade and commerce. These Jews would have come from the four directions of the earth (Acts 2:9–11). The crowd gathered, and they were amazed "because each one heard them speaking in the native language of each" (2:6). Not only were they bewildered by the sound of wind, but they also heard their native languages spoken by a group of Galileans. The narrative then goes on to list about fifteen different ethnicities that were present, and all heard the disciples speak of God's deeds of power in their own languages (2:9–11). Perplexed by this miracle, those who were present thought the disciples must be drunk. Peter quickly assured them that the men were not drunk, for it was only nine o'clock in the morning. Instead, explained Peter, this was a fulfillment of the prophecy of Joel in which God promised to pour out the Spirit in a way that makes all people, young and old, male and female, rich and poor, equal. Peter then went on to proclaim the good news of Jesus Christ, who is exalted at the right hand of God and who poured out the Spirit so that those who are present would "see and hear" (2:33).

Given that those who were present would likely have understood Aramaic or Hebrew and even Greek, the miracle of speaking other languages affirms the lordship of Jesus, the unpredictability of the Spirit, and the inauguration of the church. But it also shows that Jesus's lordship and the unity of the church are not threatened by difference; difference is embraced and affirmed, and space is created for it to enrich the whole community. The audience knew different languages; it was the church that needed to learn new languages as a practical way of opening its doors to those outside a particular group.

> It was the church that needed to learn new languages as a practical way of opening its doors beyond a particular group.

The allusions to the Babel story and its connections with Pentecost have been noted before. For example, each community was given a task: "to fill the earth" in the case of Babel and to "preach the good news throughout the earth" in the case of the disciples. Both stories speak of a dramatic divine intervention that affects people's linguistic abilities, and both narratives address the issue of the human ability to hear and understand the words spoken in a particular language. In Babel, people are unable to understand each other because God has mixed up languages, while in Jerusalem at Pentecost, people are able to hear and understand because those who had not previously known the people's languages spoke so all could understand.

Interpreters have pondered the relationship between the narrative of the Tower of Babel and the story of Pentecost. Some believe that multiplicity of languages was a punishment that resulted from human arrogance and sin at the Tower of Babel. They see Pentecost as undoing the divine punishment when God gives the gift of the Holy Spirit to restore human unity that was lost at Babel. Saint Augustine writes,

> Thanks be to God, it was to the nations that apostles were sent; if to the nations, then to all tongues. The Holy Spirit signified this, being divided in the tongues, united in the dove. Here the tongues are divided, there the dove unites them. . . . In the dove the unity, in the tongues the community of the nations. For once the tongues became discordant through pride, and then of one became many tongues. . . . If pride caused diversities of tongues, Christ's humility has united these diversities in one. The Church is now bringing together what that tower had sundered. Of one tongue there were made many; marvel not: this was the doing of pride. Of many tongues there is made one; marvel not: this was the doing of charity. For although the sounds of tongues are various, in the heart one God is invoked, one peace preserved.

Although humans after Pentecost do not speak one language, one can see that for Augustine, Babel and Pentecost stand in contrast. While Augustine recognizes multiplicity of languages, he puts a stronger accent on the unity that resulted from the work of the Spirit. Similarly, John Calvin, who sees the multiplicity of languages as a sign of divine anger and punishment for human pride, asserts that in God's goodness, communication is still possible among the nations. God's goodness was made manifest in proclaiming one gospel: "[God] has proclaimed one gospel, in all languages, through the whole world, and has induced the Apostles with the gift of tongues. Whence it has come to pass, that they who before miserably divided, have coalesced in the unity of the faith."[16] In other words, as for Augustine, John Calvin suggests that the multiplicity of languages is a divine judgment that is replaced by the unity of the proclamation of the gospel and the pouring out of the Spirit at the Pentecost. William Willimon speaks of this tradition that understands Pentecost as a reversal of Babel:

> One popular interpretation of the Pentecost is that this story signifies that Babel has been reversed (Gen 11:1–9). Human language, so confused at Babel, has been restored; community, so scattered there, has been restored. It is doubtful that Luke had this in mind. The "mighty works of God" are proclaimed only to Jews at this point. The time is not yet ripe in the story for the division between Jew and gentile to be healed. The story does not claim that there is only one language now—Luke reports that the disciples speak in a multitude of languages.[17]

Interpreters who emphasize the celebration of diversity of languages and cultures in Babel suggest that Pentecost continues this celebration of the multiplicity of languages. As noted previously, those who were present at Pentecost heard the disciples speak in the many languages of those gathered. David Smith and Barbara Maria Carvill observe the significance:

> If the more pessimistic readings of the Babel story were correct, we would expect to see a return to linguistic uniformity when healing comes, an undoing of the curse of difference. . . . But that is not what happens at all. Instead of re-creating a single language, the Spirit enables each person present to hear the wonders of God proclaimed *in his or her own language.* The gift of tongues described in the Pentecost story remarkably affirms the linguistic individuality of the hearers. Hearing, an important mark of humanity before God, is restored (cf. Gen 11:7), and in this restoration *diversity is not negated, but affirmed.*[18]

I agree that Pentecost is not antithetical to the Babel narrative: in both narratives, people speak multiple languages. But it is clear to me that the gift of the Spirit is restoring something lost at Babel. The gift of the Spirit is making communication possible. Those who were dispersed or live in diaspora are gathered again, not to reproduce uniformity, but to celebrate a unity in which diverse people can enrich one another by communicating with one another. The miraculous gift that is granted to the church here is that of speaking in tongues, which for our contemporary context could be equated with the gift of translation.

The interpretations that celebrate the multiplicity and the diversity of Babel ignore the fact that the peoples were unable to understand one another. Pentecost, however, adds something essential to the beauty of diversity and multiplicity—namely, the ability to communicate, the ability to translate. These gifts were not only necessary to share the good news with others; they were the starting point of the ideal communion that is described at the end of Acts 2, as summarized here by Letty Russell and her colleagues:

> God's gift of understanding across difference is expressed in the outpouring of the Spirit which transforms the lives of people and their communities. The Spirit does not so much create the structures and procedures, but rather breaks open structures that confine and separate people so that they can welcome difference and the challenges and opportunities for new understanding that difference brings.[19]

When we move from Babel to the Pentecost, we move from a multicultural human community in which people coexist but do not necessarily interact to an intercultural church in which people of different ethnic backgrounds flourish in communion together and in which the Spirit breaks down the walls that separate people unjustly. Fernandez suggests that the church is called to follow the work of the Spirit as evident in Pentecost, when the Spirit broke down "fixed, stable, pure, and ordered categories."[20] The work of the Spirit moves the church beyond the politics of multiculturalism and assimilation to become a hybrid community that offers and receives hospitality. Fernandez summarizes in this way:

Multiculturalism, a model that has gained wider acceptance vis-à-vis the melting pot or assimilation, continues to operate on the assumption of a pure and fixed culture juxtaposed with others and, as is often the case, leaves all forms of socio-economic inequality untouched. Hybridity [blending of diverse cultures] helps us move beyond assimilation, multiculturalism, "nativism," or postmodernistic celebration of difference that is oblivious of power relations.[21]

Through the miraculous work of the Spirit, those who have been dispersed and who have for a long time lived in diaspora can discover a sense of home when they hear their own language spoken by others who do not share their ethnic or cultural background. And those who have been gathered and settled in one location are sent out of their zone of comfort, empowered by the Spirit, to speak another language and be submerged in another culture in order to embody the good news of hospitality to other human beings whom God loves and welcomes.

Translation and Culture

Following the models of Babel and Pentecost, an intercultural church is a church that welcomes and celebrates linguistic diversity as an integral part of the biblical vision of the church. But the reconciling work that an intercultural church seeks to embody does not stop at the level of linguistic communication; the intercultural church also seeks to build bridges of understanding regarding cultural sameness and differences between its members.

Crossing linguistic barriers happens in various ways in congregations among migrant and host communities. The work of translation happens in churches that translate sermons from one language to another primarily through skilled interpreters and headphones. Various hymnals include songs that are translated in multiple languages on the same page. An essential part of the ministry of many pastors who serve migrant communities is to translate for them when immigrants need to complete paperwork or when they have to be admitted to the hospital. Second-generation immigrants translate bills, letters, contracts, and statements for their parents.

Translation is not just about language. Though knowing the words, grammar, and idioms of another language is important for building an intercultural society and an intercultural church, it is critically important to understand the cultural layers that are embedded in language. While it is important to learn other people's languages in order to show signs of hospitality, mutuality, and welcome, it is equally important to learn how to navigate cultural differences and similarities. Church leaders who are called to serve in an intercultural setting ought to receive training that helps them understand themselves and their own culture as well as acquire the tools needed to understand and engage cultures different from their own. Theological vision and biblical foundations for such a

> Translation is not just about language.

ministry are essential, and it is important to have the goodwill to reach out to those who are different culturally. Still, for these theological visions and this goodwill to be transformative, it is necessary for church leaders and church members to spend time and energy improving their intercultural competence.

Soong-Chan Rah offers a very helpful guide on how church leaders can increase their cross-cultural intelligence. Before digging deeper into some of the cultural patterns, Rah distinguishes between the external aspects of culture (music, foods, gestures, etc.) and the internal aspects of culture (ideas, beliefs, values, etc.). Following the pattern of Babel and Pentecost, for the church to become intercultural, its members need to move from a monocultural mind-set to a multicultural mind-set, where people accept each other and each other's cultural expressions. Moving along the continuum, then, these individuals would learn each other's languages and cultural expressions in order to be able to adapt and change so that they live an intercultural experience in which these members interact and influence one another. As Rah says, "Cultural intelligence for the church requires not only the recognition of different cultural expressions but the ability to accept and work within multiple cultural expressions that may end up being a part of the church community."[22]

Soong-Chan Rah lists some examples of cultural expressions, urging us not to think of them in terms of "right" and "wrong" categories. Rather, these expressions are placed on a spectrum that observers can use to identify the direction in which their own culture leans. Understanding our culture more fully empowers the church to deepen its sense of fellowship and its worship and ministry. The examples include:

- Some cultures are oriented more toward the individual, and other cultures emphasize the communal aspect of relationships.
- When something goes wrong, some cultures are concerned about external damage to their image, because shame is central to their perception of reality, while others focus more on the internalized feeling of guilt.
- How cultures view equality and hierarchy, in both explicit and implicit ways, affects how people work together and how they understand their responsibilities to one another and to their institution.
- Different cultures handle conflict differently because they operate with different in-group politics. Some are direct and confrontational, while others are indirect and avoid confrontation.
- Some cultures are task oriented, and other cultures are relationship oriented.

Reflecting on these differences will help the church understand and accomplish its mission in a way that empowers all of its members to do their part effectively and in a healthy way.

In addition to the five cultural expressions that Rah explains in his book, Duane Elmer adds five cultural expressions that a church seeking to become an intercultural community should reflect on.[23]

- While all people value time, people from different cultures value time differently. In an industrial culture, people pay attention to small units of time (seconds, minutes, and hours), whereas in an agricultural context, people care more about seasons. These differences affect how people think about planning ahead, whether they start and finish a meeting on time, and how much they get stressed about predictability and control of outcome.

- Some people look at life as a time line, shaped by a culture that tries to divide reality into categories or compartmentalize issues, events, and people. Others understand life in a holistic way, seeing people, events, and issues as intertwined and woven together like a tapestry. These differences influence how people tell their stories and how they solve problems.

- Thinking logically for the sake of solving problems follows different patterns in different cultures, and knowing one's logic pattern enables one to appreciate other people's logic patterns. Some people think in a linear way, using a chain-link logic that can be characterized as being direct and concise. Others follow a logic pattern that can be likened to an onion or a spiral, where the train of thought moves slowly from outer layers inward, slowly getting to the point. Another way of thinking logically follows a repetitious pattern, like the flower whose center is surrounded by petals that lead back to this center. While facts are important for some people when they try to solve problems, for others, facts should not be separated from emotions.

- Some cultures think of status as resulting from hard work and achievements, while other cultures think of status as something more intrinsic or ascribed to individuals based on age, experiences, family, and so on. Being aware of the difference in cultural understanding of status makes us more aware of how people greet one another or show respect in a cross-cultural setting.

- The final cultural expression discussed by Elmer has to do with worship. An intercultural church will be made of people who seek to worship God, and they will likely differ from one another on how to do that. As individuals in the church seek to follow the pattern of Babel and Pentecost—that is, to create a space for difference to flourish and a way for people to speak and understand each other's languages—new models of worship can be imagined in which all offer themselves to God using their own language and style of worship while also being receptive to the language of others and their unique style of worship, so that God may be glorified in many languages and in many forms of worship.

Discussion Questions

1. How are language and identity related or linked? What do churches need to be aware of when it comes to language and identity? Give some examples.

2. Many have interpreted the story of the Tower of Babel in Genesis 11 as a story of God's judgment on human arrogance, with God's punishment being the creation of many languages. What other interpretations of this story does the author bring out? Which interpretation resonates most with you? Why?

3. The story of Pentecost in Acts 2 is often related to the Tower of Babel story in Genesis 11. What are some of the connections? In what ways do these biblical stories inform our view of language and worship in the church?

4. What are some ways of crossing language (linguistic) barriers in churches and communities of faith?

5. Soong-Chan Rah speaks of cultural intelligence for the church and describes five ways people may approach deeper cultural understanding (see the list on pp. 141–42). Reflect on the differences described in these statements. How do you see your own church or faith community reflected in these statements? Discuss as many as time allows.

6. What gifts are present in your church or faith community that can contribute to a deeper understanding of and empathy for cultural difference and for those bringing new languages, traditions, customs, and experiences into your midst?

5

Food and Building an Intercultural Church

The covenantal relationship between God and the faith community calls for faith community members to live out a covenantal commitment with one another. Sealing the covenantal relationships with God and with others in the community happens through sharing a meal in the presence of God. Eating and drinking often accompany the establishment of covenants in the Old Testament. For example, Exodus 24 describes God's divine appearance on Mount Sinai along with the revelation of the Ten Commandments and the laws of the book of covenant. The text then reports that Moses led the people into a ceremony of establishing the covenant with God. Upon the people's commitment to obey God's commandments, Moses took the blood of the covenant, dashed it on the people, and declared, "See the blood of the covenant that the Lord has made with you in accordance with all these words" (Exod 24:8). After the establishment of the covenant, representatives of the people—Moses, Aaron, Nadab, Abihu, and seventy elders of the people of Israel—went up on the mountain, where "they beheld God, and they ate and drank" (24:11). This scene, which combines covenant making and a sacred meal, became the background for the way the Lord's Supper was celebrated in the early church. When Paul recalls the tradition of the Lord's Supper, he relates to the church in Corinth the following words of Jesus: "This cup is the new covenant in my blood" (1 Cor 11:25).

Lord's Supper and Community Building

In 1 Corinthians, Paul addresses various issues that disturbed the sense of unity among the members of the body of the Christ in Corinth. Paul cites ongoing abuses of the Lord's Supper and the inequality among the members of the church that surfaced when they came together to share the sacramental meal. Before Paul discusses how the divisions of the community were manifest in the way the Corinthians celebrated the Lord's Supper and their common meal, he makes a hermeneutical leap to connect the Corinthians with the story of the people of Israel.

Paul recalls the events of the exodus story in order to warn the Corinthians of the consequences of rebelling against God, and he includes the people of Corinth in the story of the people of Israel when he says, "Our ancestors were all under the cloud" (1 Cor 10:1). This inclusion is significant because it shows that although the people of Corinth are far in space and time from the old story, Israel's narrative is instructive to their context. Israel's narrative in this context is a story of migration. In Exodus, the people are freed from oppression, and they migrate to the promised land. Paul even goes on to interpret the crossing of the sea as an experience similar to baptism: "and all passed through the sea, and all were baptized into Moses in the cloud and in the sea" (10:1–2). Baptism is what makes individuals members of the community of God.

Paul goes on to add that they all shared in the same food and the same drink: "all ate the same spiritual food, and all drank the same spiritual drink. For they drank from the spiritual rock that followed them, and the rock was Christ" (10:3–4). Paul is writing these words in order to warn the Corinthians that despite all these gracious and benevolent acts of God toward the people, many of them suffered various forms of judgment because of their rebellion. Paul's words remind the Corinthians, who are divided, that in baptism and in sharing spiritual food and drink, the people were equal; there was no place for hierarchy. Thus, as the Corinthians hear these words of warning, they are included in the ancient story that reminds them of their migratory status and their need to remember that they are all equal before God. Allowing differences (social or economic) to divide the church is an act of idolatry and rebellion against God.

While certain kinds of eating and drinking were signs of unity and equality among the members of the faith community, other occasions of eating and drinking were rejected because they entailed idolatrous practices. For instance, Paul reminds his readers of the fact that the people of Israel who ate and drank the spiritual food and drink in the wilderness also deviated from their sole commitment to God when they worshipped the golden calf, an idolatrous act that was also accompanied by eating and drinking: "Do not become idolaters as some of them did; as it is written, 'The people sat down to eat and drink, and they rose up to play'" (10:7).

Paul then urges the Corinthians to flee from idolatry (10:14). Fleeing from worshipping idols entails not eating the meat of the sacrifices that had been offered to idols (10:18–21). The church is called to have communion in Christ and not with demons. The members of the church are different, but when they share (*koinōnia*) in the blood and the body of Christ, they become partners in the body of Christ: "The cup of blessing that we bless, is it not a sharing in the blood of Christ? The bread that we break, is it not a sharing in the body of Christ?" (10:16).

Participating in the Lord's Supper draws the church closer to God through the blood and body of Christ. This communion with God gives the church a distinct identity because its members make a choice not to partake in the surrounding culture and its idolatrous rituals. One of the ways the church becomes countercultural is when it lives in unity despite its diversity. Paul asserts, "Because there is one bread, we who are many are one body, for we all partake of the one bread" (10:17). Around the table of the Lord's Supper, cultural differences are embraced as a divine gift. Cláudio Carvalhaes underlines the role of the eucharistic table in forming a community that celebrates diversity within unity: "The eucharistic table challenges us to be together and foster our sense of struggle and who we are always becoming through these liturgies. To be together with a multiplicity of people does not mean to agree about things but to live together, not in spite of but because of our differences. The sacramental table is pressed by a multi-layered challenge, a very difficult task that demands all of us to figure out locally, within our communities, how to make sense of the multi-faceted body of Christ and the message of Jesus Christ in our world today."[1] In the Lord's Supper, believers live in communion not only with God but also with each

> One of the ways the church becomes countercultural is when it lives in unity despite its diversity.

other. Being one, being in fellowship and communion with the other, in this context means seeking not one's own advantage "but that of the other" (10:24; see also 1 Cor 8:1–13).

Concern for the welfare of others seems to have been a central problem in the Corinthian church, and that problem was manifest in the way the Corinthians distorted the meaning of the Lord's Supper and their common meal. Paul describes the situation in Corinth using varieties of words. He confronts them by saying he does not commend them for their attitude or behavior with one another when they meet. More specifically, Paul says that when they "come together it is not for the better but for the worse" (11:17) and that their meeting as a church is marked by "divisions" (11:18) and "factions" (11:19). Though they gather in order to celebrate the Lord's Supper and to share a meal together, their practices defeat the meaning of sharing (*koinōnia*) in such a sacred meal. In other words, on the surface, they appear to be "together," but they do not live out what it means to be in fellowship with one another, because all look after their own needs without considering the needs of the others: "For when the time comes to eat, each of you goes ahead with your own supper, and one goes hungry and another becomes drunk" (11:21).

The way the church in Corinth distorted the meaning of the Lord's Supper was evident in the way they handled how they ate together. Some ate too much and drank to the point of becoming drunk, while others had nothing to eat and therefore remained hungry. Panayotis Coutsoumpos describes the historical context this way:

> The church at Roman Corinth was composed of people from different social strata, the wealthy and the poor, as well as slaves and former slaves. It was customary for participants in the Lord's meal to bring from home their own food and drink. The wealthy brought so much food and drink that they could indulge in gluttony and drunkenness. The poor who came later, however, had little or nothing to bring, with the result that some of them went hungry and could not enjoy a decent meal.[2]

Paul accuses those who abused their socioeconomic privileges and showed no concern for those who were different from them of showing "contempt for the church of God" and "humiliat[ing] those who have nothing" (11:22).

To restore the meaning of fellowship in the church, Paul reminds the Corinthians of the central meaning of the Lord's Supper, namely, the self-sacrificial love that Jesus proclaimed, through which the world is reconciled with God (11:23–25). George Hunsinger elaborates on the social implications of practicing the sacrament of the Lord's Supper:

> Humiliating the poor, neglecting the needy, and conspicuous consumption in the context of the eucharistic assembly were an affront to the gospel. Christ's sacrificial sharing of himself, under the eucharistic forms of his body and blood (vv. 23–26), had social implications. It required believers not only to conform to Christ in his sacrificial self-giving (cf. Eph. 5:2), but also to rise above cultural antagonisms of religion, ethnicity, status, and gender.[3]

The church is called to witness to this love by embodying it in sharing meals with other believers in a way that honors what it means to be a church, the body of Christ. This means embodying Christ's sacrificial love toward one another and taking care to discern whether others are eating properly or eating in a way that could injure another's conscience (11:28–29). In this context, examining oneself does not just refer to one's faithfulness toward God, but it also means examining how one's actions affect others who share in the table of the Lord. The phrase "discerning the body" (1 Cor 11:29) could be referring to the body of Jesus that believers share in when they participate in the Lord's Supper, and it could very well be pointing to the body of Christ that is the church. The ambiguity here calls the church to believe that sharing in the body of Christ in the Eucharist is bound to honoring the body of Christ, the other members in the church. Honoring the body of Christ happens when one is liberated from selfishness, which can be expressed by eating with others in ways that reflect Christ's sacrificial love, which could be as simple as "when you come together to eat, wait for one another" (11:33).

Sharing Ethnic Meals

Discerning the body of Christ in the context of the intercultural church means creating space for members of the church who come from different cultural backgrounds to express their identity by sharing their ethnic meals with others who come from different cultures. Sharing food or, even better, cooking together in the context of building a community in the setting of the intercultural church can fulfill important goals.

One goal is to assure that all are fed. Food is an essential need for human survival. While thousands of people are forced to migrate because of famine and the scarcity of food resources, other communities indulge in an excess of food. With this background in mind, the church is in need of the prophetic words of Isaiah 58, which call the people to see the act of sharing food as a spiritual practice and as an act of doing justice:

> Is not this the fast that I choose:
>> to loose the bonds of injustice,
>> to undo the thongs of the yoke,
> to let the oppressed go free,
>> and to break every yoke?
> Is it not to share your bread with the hungry,

and bring the homeless poor into your house;
when you see the naked, to cover them,
and not to hide yourself from your own kin? (58:6–7)

The prophet is calling the people of God to do more than provide a food pantry or Tuesday hot meal for the homeless. Paul and Isaiah are calling for sharing meals together.

Eating together in an intercultural church, then, is a social-justice posture that meets the needs of the migrant and sojourner and transforms the "food deserts" into oases of fellowship that nourish people from different races, ethnicities, and cultural backgrounds with the same healthy and varied diet. Doing justice and offering hospitality to the other is intertwined with loving God, as Cláudio Carvalhaes reminds us:

> A table grounded in the ethics of justice will honor God and strive to honor every human being in their very daily lives and the ability to live with means for a dignified life. The Eucharist table challenges us to ask ourselves as individuals and communities: what are we to do with this sacrament? This table is deeply marked by the ethics of responsibility where the face of the other in/evolves every step of my liturgy before God.[4]

Sharing meals with one another is formative in strengthening the impulse of church members to give and receive. Giving and receiving are not measured by quantity but reflect acts of hospitality and show the agency of the parties involved. They also show people being at peace with being vulnerable and dependent on the goodness of the other.

A second goal of cooking and eating together in the church is to foster a community that seeks to embrace, understand, and be transformed by cultural differences. Massimo Montanari unpacks various important insights about the role that food could play in forming a community:

> Like spoken language, the food system contains and conveys the culture of its practitioner; it is the repository of traditions and of collective identity. It is therefore an extraordinary vehicle of self-representation and of cultural exchange—a means of establishing identity, to be sure, but also the first way of entering into contact with a different culture. Eating the food of the "other" is easier, it would seem, than decoding the other's language. Far more than spoken language itself, food can serve as a mediator between different cultures, opening methods of cooking to all manner of invention, cross-pollination, and contamination. The two notions of identity and exchange, often called up when dealing with food culture, are contrasted at times as though the exchange, that is, the confrontation of different identities, were itself the obstacle to the preservation of those identities, and of the cultural heritage that each society recognizes in its own past.[5]

The food system contains and conveys the culture of the practitioner.

Food as an expression of identity allows the different communities that form an intercultural church to encounter each other's cultural heritages. As Montanari notes, one might not know the other's language, but one can communicate with the other by eating the food of the other and by offering one's food to the other. In this way, food is a site of exchange of cultures. Furthermore, food underlines an important aspect of how communities negotiate the sameness and difference between the multiple cultures that are part of the church. Think, for example, of how people experience similarities and differences in the smell of ethnic foods. Montanari suggests also that food is a helpful way to talk about identity preservation and innovation. Although one may associate a particular cuisine with a particular region or culture, that same food in that same region may be cooked differently by different people in different families. Food creates a tasty way of talking about continuity and change in culture.

Food and Peace Building

Shared meals that accompany covenant making between the migrant and the host create a space for the two parties to offer and receive hospitality. Such a communal activity in which one party extends a table to those who are different becomes a sign of seeking the well-being of the other. Covenant initiates a mutual relationship of promises and responsibility, and sharing food seals this relationship by adding a concrete taste of the uniqueness, generosity, and commitment of the parties involved.

In the story of Isaac and the Philistines, which I discussed in the second chapter, food and covenant intersect in powerful ways. In this episode of the story, there is truth telling, reversal of the hospitality paradigm, and a transformation of conflict.

Recall that because Isaac lied to the Philistines about his wife Rebecca and because of his growing prosperity, the Philistines ask Isaac to leave, saying, "Go away from us; you have become too powerful for us" (Gen 26:16). When Isaac leaves, the Philistines seek to put a cap on his prosperity by filling with dirt the wells that Abraham or Isaac had dug. This act is especially distressing because it is a time of famine, and water is scarce. Isaac, like many migrants, might have experienced a feeling of being cut off, separated from family and home. In the midst of confusion, God assures Isaac, "I am the God of your father Abraham; do not be afraid, for I am with you" (26:24). God's presence and promise of blessings prepare Isaac for the following episode, in which the rejected offers hospitality, and the guest becomes the host.

The king of the Philistines, Abimelech, goes to Isaac, accompanied by his adviser, Ahuzzath, and by Phicol, the commander of his army (Gen 26:26). Before they have a chance to say anything, Isaac confronts them and speaks truth to them: "Why have you come to me, seeing that you hate me and have sent me away from you?" (26:27). Isaac confronts his guests with the truth as he sees it. Though he feels hated and rejected by the Philistines, he chooses not to respond violently to their behavior. This choice does not in any way compromise how Isaac describes the situation and how the Philistines' awful treatment makes him feel.

Yet Isaac is also open to hear the Philistines out. The Philistines in turn respond to Isaac and explain the situation from their perspective: "We see plainly that the LORD has been with you; so we say, let there be an oath between you and us, and let us make a covenant with you so that you will do us no harm, just as we have not touched you and have done to you nothing but good and have sent you away in peace. You are now the blessed of the LORD" (26:28–29). They recognize that the Lord is with Isaac and that the Lord has blessed Isaac. These two aspects are parallel to what God said to Isaac in the vision (26:24). Thus, the text portrays the Philistines as ones who recognize the work of the Lord in the other. As a result, they seek to establish a covenant with Isaac. The Philistines are not only portrayed as people who are capable of recognizing the presence of God with the other, but they also recognize that Isaac's prosperity does not have to be perceived as a threat. They can coexist. Furthermore, the Philistines are not passive recipients of Isaac's version of the story. Instead, they also tell the story from their perspective, and thus they seek mutual respect and reciprocal peace.

Isaac does not dispute their version of the story. It is possible that the episode of the wells is not integral to the story, so the Philistines believe they have not harmed Isaac and have sent him in peace. At any rate, such an honest confrontation in which there was a space for each side to narrate the story from their perspective leads to fellowship between Isaac and the Philistines. Before they officially swear to one another and establish a covenant of peace between them, Isaac puts together a feast for them. At the beginning of the story, Isaac was the one who migrated because of famine; that is, he had to move and sojourn in the land of the Philistines for his own survival. Isaac was the guest, the outsider, the sojourner, and the migrant, while the Philistines were the insiders and played the role of the hosts. We have a reversal here. When Isaac sets up the banquet for the Philistines, he becomes the guest who hosts the host, the outsider who shows hospitality to the insiders. This banquet is more than a simple meal; it is a significant meal in that it accompanies the covenant. Even more significant is that the meal reveals the fuzziness of the boundaries between the insider and outsider, the migrant and the host.

Quite often, people assume that generosity and hospitality are only the work of insiders, and in many cases, this is true. But it is a great blessing when the insiders or the hosts are also open to receiving hospitality from the migrant and the guest. Inviting people to tell their stories while sharing a meal with others can be a significant way of building authentic fellowship in the church. One time, as I was leading a Bible study on migration and the Bible, we started by telling stories about how each of us got to where we currently live. Telling these stories not only preserves them but also gives us a real opportunity to walk into each other's lives in a deep and meaningful way. We all realize that we or our ancestors have been sojourners, migrants, and outsiders in

> But it is a great blessing when the insiders or the hosts are also open to receiving hospitality from the migrant and the guest.

one way or another. This recognition liberates us from rigid categories of us and them, insiders and outsiders.

Sharing a meal for the sake of reconciliation and peace building between different communities that have experienced conflict, hatred, racism, alienation, and marginalization creates space for people to be honest and transparent. Such exchanges over meals could include stories of mutuality and hospitality and also painful stories of hatred and exclusion. This is not an easy process; it may be painful and risky, but it is necessary. Soong-Chan Rah in his book *Many Colors* writes,

> Unable to deal with a tainted racial history, churches continue to operate on the norm of segregation. . . . The church needs to examine its history—to both remember and to lament the stories of pain that are endemic to our experience and story as a church. . . . Our ability to move beyond our differences and conflicts rests in our ability to deal with the differences and conflicts in our past as well as in our present—otherwise we are merely sweeping reality and history under the rug in order to feel comfortable in our ignorance. . . . In order to move forward toward cultural intelligence, the sharing of our stories has to be a part of our journey.[6]

People who participate in telling their stories and those who listen to the stories should be prepared to handle painful and shameful memories. Such storytelling cannot guarantee a safe space, but it will create sacred space that leads to transformation. In telling stories, we lament the stories of pain that are endemic to our experience and story as a church. We realize that we do not walk into the past alone but are accompanied by the rest of the body of Christ, whose members listen carefully and offer encouragement. Above all, creating a space for stories to be told requires relying on the healing power of the Holy Spirit. When there is courage to tell and listen to people's narratives, the church creates a space for the Spirit of God to empower the church to move from pain, shame, and oppression into the realm of the kingdom of God, where healing, justice, love, and reconciliation reflect the work of our Prince of Peace.

Food and Integration

The book of Ruth is a story of migration in which the shortage and availability of food shape the course of events and the actions of the characters. The narrative begins with a shortage of food that drives Naomi and Elimelech to migrate from Bethlehem, which ironically means "house of bread," to seek survival in a foreign land: "In the days when the judges ruled, there was a famine in the land, and a certain man of Bethlehem in Judah went to live in the country of Moab, he and his wife and two sons" (1:1). After the tragic deaths of Naomi's husband, Elimelech, and her two sons, Mahlon and Chilion, Naomi decides to return to Judah because she has heard that God has provided food for the people: "Then she started to return with her daughters-in-law from the country of Moab, for she had heard in the country of Moab that the LORD had considered his people and given them food" (1:6). One of Naomi's daughters-in-law, Orpah, stays behind in

Moab, but Naomi's Moabite daughter-in-law, Ruth, decides to migrate with Naomi to Naomi's homeland. When Naomi and Ruth finally reach Bethlehem, the text notes that it is "the beginning of the barley harvest" (1:22).

As Ruth and Naomi settle in Bethlehem, food continues to play an important role in the development of the story. Ruth, the foreigner, informs her mother-in-law that she will go out to the fields to "glean among the ears of grain" (2:2). She does so and eventually ends up gleaning in the field of Naomi's relative Boaz. Because Ruth is a foreigner, she must work behind the regular workers and gather what has been left behind. She works tirelessly all day without resting. Boaz notices and extends an invitation to Ruth to glean only in his fields and orders the young men not to bother her. If she gets thirsty she is to "go to the vessels and drink from what the young men have drawn" (2:9). In addition to offering her water, Boaz also invites Ruth to eat with his harvesters: "At mealtime Boaz said to her, 'Come here, and eat some of this bread, and dip your morsel in the sour wine.' So she sat beside the reapers, and he heaped up for her some parched grain. She ate until she was satisfied, and she had some left over" (2:14).

Upon her return to her mother-in-law and before any words are said between Ruth and Naomi, the text reports that "her mother-in-law saw how much she had gleaned. Then she took out and gave her what was left over after she herself had been satisfied" (2:18). Later, a rendezvous takes place between Ruth and Boaz on the threshing floor after Boaz has had something to eat and drink (3:3, 7), and it ends with Boaz giving Ruth a gift of six measures of barley (3:15). But more than that, Boaz promises to act as "next-of-kin" for Ruth (3:13), essentially assuring her, a foreigner, a place in his family.

In the story of Ruth, food plays a significant role in integrating this foreigner into the society of Bethlehem. In this way, the story provides a recipe for nurturing intercultural communities and churches. For integration to happen, hosts and migrants who possess different kinds of privileges must see that they have something significant to offer one another. The generosity and hospitality of Boaz offer an alternative to the politics of fear and scarcity. His recognition of the foreigner is an example of using one's privilege to make space for the alien other to be part of the community. At the same time, the faithfulness, resilience, and generosity of the migrant Ruth challenge misconceptions about migrants as a threat to the well-being of the society. This story is an example of how food can be an important medium through which the different agents of an intercultural community can recognize each other as human beings worthy of respect and can express hospitality and generosity to each other.

As noted earlier, Naomi and Ruth return to Bethlehem at the beginning of the barley harvest. Although she is a foreigner, Ruth takes the initiative to go out to the field in order to glean grain for herself and her mother-in-law so they will survive. She takes the initiative, knowing that ancient Israel has a law or a custom requiring harvesters to leave the forgotten sheaves of grain in the field for the widow, the orphan, and the stranger to pick up (Lev 23:22; Deut 24:19–22). Yet she also understands the risks of being in need of food and at the mercy of other human beings. She has to work "behind someone in whose sight I may find favor" (2:2). Katharine Doob Sakenfeld notes, "Ruth, by contrast to Naomi, dares to take initiative to support the two of them, even though her words show that she anticipates possible resistance to her presence."[7] The need for food is a core expression of human vulnerability, and it also drives the resilience needed to take any risk to meet that need. Sometimes meeting that need also means crossing boundaries to be with other human beings who are capable of being compassionate or excluding the foreigner and the alien, depriving them of sharing.

It is fortuitous that Ruth ends up gleaning in the field of Boaz, a relative of Elimelech, Naomi's deceased husband. Upon his arrival at the field, he notices Ruth and asks the supervisor of the harvesters about her identity (2:3–4). The supervisor's report highlights two important aspects of Ruth's identity. First, he identifies her as the Moabite (and thus a foreigner) who has returned with Naomi (a relative of Boaz) from the land of Moab (2:6). Not mentioning her by name may highlight her foreignness and otherness. His statement that she is the one who came with Naomi from the land of Moab also may indicate that although she is a foreigner, she is seeking integration in this new society. The second aspect of Ruth's identity that the supervisor highlights is her work ethic: "She has been on her feet from early this morning until now, without resting even for a moment" (2:7). This verse has multiple textual problems in Hebrew, leading scholars to understand it in three different ways. Some scholars suggest that the text means Ruth is still standing, waiting for Boaz to grant her permission to glean in his field. Other scholars think Ruth has already started gleaning, and Boaz notices her only because she is taking a break. A final understanding of the verse suggests that Ruth received permission to glean from the supervisor and has been working hard without taking a single break. The first reading is the least plausible one, but it shows that Ruth is patient and resilient; the latter two proposals are more plausible and underline the fact that Ruth is hardworking and perseveres.

Boaz is a prominent rich man who uses his privilege to show hospitality to the vulnerable, foreign, diligent Moabite woman, Ruth. He first offers her protection by commanding his workers not to harass her (2:9). Later in the chapter, Boaz seeks more than physical protection; he asks the workers not to rebuke or humiliate her (2:15–16). Furthermore, he gives her instructions on where and how to glean. He also carves out a space for her in the social circle of workers so she will not be left out. What is remarkable about Boaz's strategy to integrate Ruth is the way he offers her water from the same vessels out of which his young men drink. That is to say, she has become part of this group and has access to some of their resources. Workers who labor in the field in the heat of day will always be in dire need of fresh water to be able to continue working. By offering Ruth a drink of water, Boaz empowers her to continue her diligent work. His invitation to her to share in the bread and the sour wine reserved for the harvesters signifies hospitality and inclusion.

Boaz's provision of water and food to Ruth the Moabite stands in clear contrast to the way the Moabites treated the Israelites who were migrating from Egypt to the land of the promise.[8] According to the Deuteronomic law, the Moabites were excluded from becoming part of the assembly of the Lord. The reason behind this exclusion, according to Deuteronomy 23:3–4, is that the Moabites as well as the Ammonites "did not meet you with food and water on your journey out of Egypt." In other words, if the reason behind the exclusion of the Moabites from the assembly of the Lord is their inhospitality to the sojourning Israelites, the inclusion of Ruth into the assembly of the Lord happens in this narrative by way of allowing her to partake in the food and the drink offered to the workers in the field. Boaz's generosity breaks the cycle of exclusion. The cycle of exclusion had already been broken when the Moabites welcomed the Israelites Elimelech and Naomi and their sons, and it was also broken when Ruth showed faithfulness toward her mother-in-law.

The hospitality that Boaz, the insider, shows to the outsider Ruth by providing water and food surrounds an important exchange of dialogue between Boaz and Ruth. Ruth herself is amazed by his acts of generosity and wonders aloud, "Why have I found favor in your sight, that you should take notice of me, when I am a foreigner?" (2:10). This verse is intriguing in Hebrew because the words translated "take notice" and "foreigner" are from the same root (*nkr*). That is, a foreigner is one who is not recognized. But the story of Ruth indicates that sharing food with foreigners is a concrete way of recognizing them as human beings who are worthy of dignity and honor. Offering water and food to outsiders is a way of recognizing and taking responsibility for their needs. This observation can be strengthened by noting that when Ruth returns to her mother-in-law with plenty of grain, Naomi exclaims, "Blessed be the man who took notice of you" (2:19). Naomi uses the same root (*nkr*) in order to signify that allowing a foreigner to glean and offering her extra food are acts of welcome and recognition of the foreigner. Those who do such acts of hospitality are blessed by the Lord.

It is also intriguing to note that Boaz's acts seem like an initiation of generosity and hospitality to the foreigner when they are, in fact, a response to the faithfulness, loyalty, and acts of generosity and resilience of the migrant herself. In his response to Ruth's question in 2:10, Boaz explains that he is impressed with Ruth's acts of faithfulness toward Naomi and her willingness to accept the risk that comes with her loyalty to her mother-in-law, even if this means going to be with a people she does not know (2:11–12). Later in the narrative, Boaz further recognizes Ruth's actions as acts of faithfulness (Heb. *khesed*; cf. 3:10; 1:8), and he asserts that all the people of Bethlehem know that Ruth is a woman of valor (Heb. *khayil*; cf. 3:11 and 2:1).

Ruth is in many ways a foreigner in need of recognition, but what gets her noticed and makes her known is her faithfulness in going to the field to find food for herself and her mother-in-law. Just as Boaz expresses his hospitality by way of offering food and water to Ruth, it is important to note that Ruth also manifests faithfulness toward her mother-in-law. She eats much of the parched grain Boaz gives her, but she also saves some for her mother-in-law (2:14). Ruth the migrant, the alien, shows hospitality to her mother-in-law, although they are in Naomi's home country. Indeed, Ruth the foreigner receives a gift of food from Boaz, who seeks to integrate her fully into his family and society by marrying her. This incorporation into the family will lead to her becoming the great-grandmother of King David.

Ruth's actions also make her an agent who fills the emptiness experienced by Naomi, the migrant who has lost everything. The Hebrew text uses the word for "to make empty" (*riq*) to show the contrast. In 1:21, Naomi laments, saying, "I went away [to Moab] full, / but the Lord has brought me back [to Bethlehem] *empty*" (italics added). In 3:17, Ruth describes Boaz's generosity by saying, "He gave me these six measures of barley, for he said, 'Do not go back to your mother-in-law *empty*-handed.'"

Sharing food is an act of hospitality. When communities do this, they start building intercultural communities in which cycles of exclusion can be broken. Such sharing signals a new way for the different individuals and communities to relate to one another as agents of social solidarity who are capable of expressing their faithfulness by meeting the needs of the other.

Note: A liturgy for gathering around the table is provided in the appendix.

Discussion Questions

1. In your opinion why does the sharing of food and drink often accompany covenant ceremonies in the Bible?
2. How does the apostle Paul's description of the Lord's Supper in 1 Corinthians 10 recall or connect the reader to the Israelites' experience in Exodus?
3. What abuses of the holy meal does Paul say were happening in the Corinthian church? What does he suggest needs to happen to assure that the meal is received properly?

4. What benefits can come from sharing meals in an intercultural church?
5. How can stories and storytelling be incorporated into meals of reconciliation and peace building?
6. How does food figure prominently in the story of Ruth, who comes to Israel as a migrant Moabite? What ultimately happens to Ruth, and what does this outcome say about our welcome of others in the church?
7. Can you imagine what a meal and a time of storytelling might look like in your church or faith community? What kind of meals would be cooked and served? What are the practices you would include in order to expand the table and deepen fellowship?
8. Have you used the meal liturgy that is included in the appendix? How did people experience it? What would you change in it in order to make it suitable for your context?

6

The Witness of the Intercultural Church

An intercultural church is a missional church. When Christians from different cultural, linguistic, ethnic, and racial backgrounds worship God by gathering around the word and the sacraments of baptism and the Eucharist, when they are in fellowship together to deepen their relationships as members of the body of Christ, they respond to God's saving grace and embody God's mission in the world. According to Lois Barrett,

> A missional church is a church that is shaped by participating in God's mission, which is to set things right in a broken, sinful world, to redeem it, and to restore it to what God has always intended for the world. Missional churches see themselves not so much sending, as being sent. A missional congregation lets God's mission permeate everything that the congregation does—from

worship to witness to training members for discipleship. It bridges the gap between outreach and congregational life, since, in its life together, the church is to embody God's mission.[1]

The description of the intercultural church that I have offered in the preceding chapters resonates with this definition of a missional church. An intercultural church seeks to live up to the biblical vision of the church evident in Pentecost and in the eschatological vision of Revelation, where cultural, ethnic, linguistic, and racial differences are not rejected and do not hinder this diverse community from worshipping God and serving one another and the world that surrounds them. When the church becomes intercultural, it does not just preach reconciliation to the world; it lives it, and it lets God's reconciling mission in the world permeate everything it does.

> When the church becomes intercultural, it does not just preach reconciliation to the world, it lives it.

In this chapter, however, I will focus on the witness of the intercultural church in relation to three issues. These three emphases relate to recent waves of migrations and to the questions that the movements of these communities have brought to the fore:

1. What particular questions of pastoral care arise in an intercultural church where recent migrants or

172

second-generation migrants occupy a significant part of the faith community?

2. How is the work of integrating migrants an important part of envisioning intercultural churches and societies?

3. What impact can intercultural churches have on inter-religious encounters and dialogue?

An Intercultural Church: A Space for Healing and Orientation

The church is called by God to be a sign of hope in the midst of despair, a place of healing in the depth of brokenness, and a guide in times of disorientation. Being a sign of God's reign in the world begins by trusting in God's healing grace, by living out the hope that God is at work transforming the world that God loves, and by being oriented toward loving God fully by being in fellowship with other human beings who are different cultur-ally, linguistically, racially, socioeconomically, and ethnically. As a church seeks to become an intercultural church, it needs to reflect biblically, theologically, and practically on how to be this sign of hope in light of the history of conquest and colonialism that has pushed many people away from their lands; in light of the history of forced migration, enslavement, and racism; and in light of the current waves of migration of communities that are escaping poverty, civil wars, and natural disasters.

The church, therefore, needs to address the needs of its members who are longing for healing from the traumatic experiences they have endured and who yearn for a sense of orientation in the midst of losses and changes they have gone through. Even communities that have not experienced movements across national borders in recent decades—for social, economic, political, or personal reasons—need healing and reorientation in their lives. Many pastoral-care challenges and opportunities emerge in any church setting. But an intercultural church made up of different people with different experiences can also provide care for new immigrants who have been forced to cross or traveled across borders.

One of the central challenges and opportunities that recent migrants, asylum seekers, or refugees face is the loss of context and the need to construct a new context. Brenda Consuelo Ruiz suggests, "Pastoral care and counseling of immigrants should preferably be the work of communities rather than individuals. Embracing newcomers, making them feel part of the family of God and of local families, is the best care that can be provided."[2] As migrants seek to figure out the relation between their old context and their new context, churches can "become therapeutic communities where immigrants feel welcome and cared for."

Martin Walton suggests that language and cultural differences trouble migrants but that their stories usually point to other layers of their struggle to make sense of their life:

> Although the stories began there and then, that is, somewhere at some point in time, a significant part of the story was marked by disruption of the familiar or usual relation to time and space. The loss of context or the experience of passage without a sense of locality were part of the (traumatic) experiences of migration. And

even the here and now of the present situation was often one marked by an ambivalent relation to the new context, to the locality but also to the time dimension.[3]

Walton then provides a model for pastoral care that addresses the experiences of loss and ambivalence that surround migrants, refugees, and asylum seekers. In this model, pastoral care evolves along three dimensions: space, time, and transcendence.

Concern around "space" is reflected in the question "Where am I?" It refers to both the "natural" place (the country, the geography, the landscape, etc.) and the social space (relationships, status, orientation). When people migrate, their sense of connectedness to a particular place is destabilized if not shattered, and they go through the pain of separation from familiar localities and people. They leave family and friends behind, along with familiar aspects of that space, such as noises, smells, food, and traditions. Even though the world today is better connected through the internet and social media, people who are displaced experience "detachment and disconnection."[4] Walton and other scholars of pastoral care suggest that migrants who face the disturbing loss of familiarity and connectedness should be empowered to recount and preserve memories of the space that was once called home and then should be helped to imagine a better life in the new place. For a migrant church or an intercultural church to become a space of healing and orientation, it must create intentional spaces in worship and fellowship practices for people to recall and talk about the places they left behind, and about their hopes for and struggles in making their new place a home.

Concern around time is reflected in the question "When am I?" Time here does not just refer to hours, days, and years, but it also refers to the change and continuity that migrants experience over time. Time, in other words, refers to "the degree to which one can identify (with) her- or himself in the dialectic of things subject to change and things that remain sufficiently familiar."[5] Many migrants use phrases like "I had to start all over again" in referring to the disruption of the story line of their life. They have to look for a job, and they have to put time and effort into learning the skills of their new career. For individuals to recover from the disruption of time, they need to find ways to resolve their relationship with the past. Whether they experienced success or failure in the past, they need to reflect on how these experiences shaped their identity so they can create room for continuity and reflect on how to let go of the past, thus creating room to embrace change. The open future has its potential, which can be inspiring or overwhelming. When everything is possible, life can be challenging. Still, the way is open for opportunities to experience human solidarity with church members and to trust in divine providence.

The third dimension that Walton highlights as an essential component for pastoral care among migrants is "transcendence." This dimension is concerned with the question "From where and to where am I?" This question does not refer to the physical movement of the human being, although this is important, as was discussed above in connection with space, but it rather refers to the origin and meaning of life. Walton suggests that the question about transcendence could be thought of in relation to "the dialect of reception and contribution," which ultimately emphasizes the purpose of life, granted that reflecting on the purpose of life is not separated from thinking about the origin of life. Although migration poses many challenges and disruptions, the resilient faith of migrants is evident. In the face of disorientation and losses, they trust in God's healing power, and in the face of the unknown future, they rely on God's providence to guide them through what is new and unfamiliar. Pastoral care in an intercultural church would do well to create spaces in worship and fellowship practices for spiritualities of lament and spiritualities of praise and thanksgiving to be expressed before God and others.

> In a missional intercultural church, migrants are not just recipients of care; they can make tremendous contributions to the spiritual formation of any congregation.

In a missional intercultural church, migrants are not just recipients of care; they can make tremendous contributions to the spiritual formation of any congregation in which they participate. But these contributions may be suffocated by too much hospitality from host communities or by a distorted self-image on the part of migrant communities who think they have nothing to offer. Gemma Tulud Cruz offers many valuable insights on the contribution of migration and migrants to spiritual and faith formation in an intercultural church.[6] She writes that migrant ways of life enrich Christian spirituality in four different ways:

1. **Courageous hope.** The decision to leave one's home country and family is agonizing and painful. The most difficult reality about making this decision is that these human beings are choosing between two painful realities—leaving home and facing an unknown future. Despite the expected perils of the journey, migrants continue to hold steadfastly onto hope in a better life. This "courageous hope" is a "hope that continues to believe and opens itself to possibilities of transformation that can never be fully spoken of."[7]

2. **Creative resistance.** People migrate because they face threats (natural, economic, political) that put their life in danger, and they also face oppression and racism in the forms of closed borders or segregated refugee camps. In their creative and imaginative strategies of resisting oppression, migrants combine active and passive ways of relating to power. They "fight against oppression in their quest for full humanity and liberation," and they use jokes, "songs, rituals, codes, and euphemisms that usually come from their folk cultures."[8]

3. **Steadfast faith.** Migrants constantly invoke faith and trust in God as they embark on their sojourn. Their practices and rituals reflect their deep love for God and the church. The experience of walking through deserts and crossing continents by land, air, or water transforms the meaning of life for them, and the relationship with God becomes central to who they are. Attending church on Sundays is an expression of their faith journey, not

simply as individuals, but also as a community. They use icons, hymns, biblical passages, or figures to help them make sense of their uprootedness. Their faith is also reflected in the ways they receive help from the church, as well as in the many things they offer one another as they create a holding environment for newcomers. Their faith is thus active and sacrificial.[9]

4. **Festive community spirit.** Church meetings, Bible study, and eucharistic celebrations are usually followed by festive meals shared by the body of Christ. These festive communal meals manifest some characteristics of migrant communities that can be instructive spiritually. These meals maintain a tension between, on the one hand, preserving identity by experiencing the smell and taste of a "home" food with a community from the same culture and, on the other hand, expressing generosity and hospitality by leaving room at the table for people from different cultures.[10]

Integration of Migrants in Society and Church

In the first chapter of this book, I noted that an intercultural church is a body of followers of Jesus Christ who come from different cultural, ethnic, linguistic, and racial backgrounds and are called by God to be the body of Christ that celebrates diversity in worship, fellowship, and ministry. An intercultural church moves beyond monocultural churches, which function under the model of assimilation in some cases and the model of separation in other cases. It also moves beyond multicultural churches, where people coexist without deep interaction between the different groups that make up the church. In the previous chapters, I have described the foundations that I believe the Bible lays down for why an intercultural church is a reflection of biblical ecclesiology. Here I return to the issue of integration, because the intentional work of building bridges of trust and mutuality between people who are different is an essential feature of the church and becomes a witness to the world, which is divided and suffers from enmity. When Christians take seriously the call to worship, fellowship, and serve with those who are different, and when they realize how much work and sacrifice it takes to live this calling, they witness to the work of Jesus, who

> came and proclaimed peace to you who were far off and peace to those who were near; for through him both of us have access in one Spirit to the Father. So then you are no longer strangers and aliens, but you are citizens with the saints and also members of the household of God, built upon the foundation of the apostles and prophets, with Christ Jesus himself as the cornerstone. In him the whole structure is joined together and grows into a holy temple in the Lord; in whom you also are built together spiritually into a dwelling place for God. (Eph 2:17–22)

Daniel Schipani has developed a diagram of five possible cross-cultural orientations that characterize relationships between migrant and host communities. These orientations include accommodation, separation, segregation, assimilation, and integration. Schipani treats accommodation as the initial and transitional relation between the host and migrant communities. In this stage, the host community, or those who possess power, use their privilege for the sake of outsiders: "The hosts will ideally exercise *power for* (that is, in favor of) the immigrants in light of key values such as compassion, hospitality, respect, and service. Theologically viewed, from the perspective of the hosts, the focal motif is *welcoming the stranger* (as welcoming God, the Christ)."[11] After some time, both the host and the migrant communities start to renegotiate their relationship in light of new circumstances, such as the growing familiarity of the outsiders with their new habitat. The way host and migrant communities handle power affects the direction their relationship will take. People who are from the dominant culture sometimes exercise their power against those who are culturally different from them, and thus they reject minority cultures and force them into segregation. On other occasions, the less-dominant culture chooses separation in order to preserve its identity, so its people can exercise the power and agency they have in order to resist assimilation.

The other two cross-cultural orientations are also shaped by how power relations are negotiated between migrant and host communities. Sometimes the dominant culture exercises power over less-dominant cultures by treating assimilation and the erosion of difference as conditions for welcoming the stranger. Sometimes, minority cultures adopt assimilation in order to survive or succeed. When migrant and host communities use their power for and with the other, there is a greater possibility that the cross-cultural matrix of integration will be lived out. Integration is marked by the mutuality of continuity and change, of giving and receiving. Daniel Schipani explains the role power relations play in the process of integration: "In the process of integration, host communities and immigrants consider each other as equal in power and are open to mutual cultural enrichment as well as correction. The power dynamic is primarily collaborative, or *power with*. Key undergirding values are, then, solidarity, mutuality, diversity, and creativity. And the main theological motif is reconciliation and fashioning 'new humanity.'"[12]

> Integration is marked by the mutuality of continuity and change, of giving and receiving.

Theological work surrounding the relationship between host and migrant communities should focus on deconstructing ideologies that lead to domination or demonization of the other. Emphases should be placed on the equality of all human beings before God because they are created in God's image and because they are all equal in Christ. Each culture has good things to offer, and each has things that need to be critiqued. Each culture has something to offer and at the same time needs the other.

When the church puts these theological convictions into practice and embodies them by becoming an intercultural body of Christ where difference is welcomed and celebrated and where power is shared in service to God and each other, then the church is better equipped to deal with religious difference outside the church. Claiming and experiencing peace with otherness within the church empowers the church to reflect God's love and compassion to the religious other beyond its immediate community.

An Intercultural Church: Witness to the Religious Other

We struggle with religious pluralism and with diversity within the same faith tradition. Some might be so strongly grounded in their own articulation of faith that they reject others who believe differently. Other people are willing to give up the particularities of their faith tradition as a way of promoting tolerance. But both approaches make interreligious or ecumenical dialogue difficult, for different reasons. The former builds barriers to dialogue because it assumes that there is no chance for others who believe differently to hold some truth or goodness in their conviction. This approach might lead to a monologue rather than a dialogue, and the faith of the other is constructed as a foil to prove the truth of one's own faith. This approach might also lead to a strict way of thinking about evangelism and mission in narrow terms of coercive conversions. The latter approach also blocks dialogue because it assumes that tolerance happens only by way of focusing on what is common and by avoiding the peculiarity of each faith tradition. This approach reduces one's faith and the faith of the other to some universal values and leads to a subtle reductionist aggression toward one's own faith tradition and the faith of the other.

The need to address the way Christians relate to the religious other has intensified in this season of world politics. Political discourse in populist movements in the United States and Europe has moved in the direction of bigotry, showing hatred and inhospitality toward Muslims and migrants. Political propaganda has focused on building walls instead of focusing on building bridges of understanding and appreciation for the other. Some political campaigns have focused on fueling environments of fear and have shown little concern for the needs of the migrant or the religious other. While some approaches tend to demonize the religious other out of their fear of the unknown, other approaches tend to play down difference in religious identities or beliefs, assuming that this posture would bring peace and well-being to the society. The challenge, then, is how to be grounded in one's own faith tradition while at the same time showing respect for, love of, and cooperation with those who hold different religious beliefs. Matthew Kaemingk advocates a new way to relate to the religious other. He calls this new way Christian pluralism. In Christian pluralism, followers of Jesus are called to celebrate cultural and religious diversity as a gift from God, and while they are grounded in their own faith, they are exhorted to show compassion and hospitality to the religious other. Kaemingk writes, "Christian pluralism is a serious exploration about how to show love, hospitality, and justice across . . . deep differences."[13]

The following sections will discuss specific biblical texts that deal with religious difference in order to provide a framework for how Christians could relate to the religious other. This framework will be informed by two questions: First, how do we negotiate boundaries for ourselves as we seek to be grounded in our own faith tradition without becoming coercive and violent to those who hold beliefs that differ from our own? And second, how do we build bridges of dialogue and solidarity with the religious other without losing our own religious identity?

Grounded in Faith and Open to the Other

Solomon's prayer in 1 Kings 8 offers important insights for the intercultural church that wrestles with how to relate to the religious other. After bringing the ark of the covenant to the newly finished temple, the glory of the Lord filled the house. Then Solomon led the assembled people of Israel in a prayer in order to dedicate the temple for the worship of the God of Israel. The text then reports that

> Solomon stood before the altar of the LORD in the presence of all the assembly of Israel, and spread out his hands to heaven. He said, "O LORD, God of Israel, there is no God like you in heaven above or on earth beneath, keeping covenant and steadfast love for your servants who walk before you with all their heart. . . . [W]hen a foreigner, who is not of your people Israel, comes from a distant land because of your name—for they shall hear of your great name, your mighty hand, and your outstretched arm—when a foreigner comes and prays toward this house, then hear in heaven your dwelling place, and do according to all that the foreigner calls to

you, so that all the peoples of the earth may know your name and fear you, as do your people Israel, and so that they may know that your name has been invoked on this house that I have built." (8:22–23, 41–43)

While Solomon prays to his own God, holds a unique place for his deity, and operates out of the theological framework of the covenant, he creates space for non-Israelites who, volitionally, pray to YHWH and make pilgrimage to Jerusalem. Solomon intercedes for them and shows concern for their needs. And if the non-Israelites turn to God in prayer, Solomon asks God to listen to their prayers and "do according to all that the foreigner calls to you" (8:43).

This passage from 1 Kings provides an alternative to the politics of fear and to the politics of anger and mistrust. As a politician and as a king, Solomon, in his prayer dedicating the temple, remembers the foreigner, the outsider, the religious other. Solomon here does not seek to stir fears or insecurities about the future among his people. Rather, he intercedes in behalf of those who will come to Jerusalem in order to bring their prayers before YHWH, the God of Israel. Prayers for those who are targeted by offensive political discourse are a significant responsibility for the church. Activism that opposes all forms of bigotry and exclusion is needed. When we pray in behalf of the other, we empathize with them and realize that the task is bigger than ourselves. When we urge God to listen to their prayers, we commit ourselves to a posture of trust as the foreigner, the stranger, and the religious other exercise their own agency in prayers and pleas for justice.

A key difference between the dedicatory prayer of Solomon and the political discourse we hear these days, even by those who try to gain more votes by appealing to Christian voters, lies in the genre of prayer, which is quite different from political speeches and presidential debates. In prayers, even the king, the head of the state, realizes that he is ultimately not in control. This is evident in the posture of Solomon, who "stood before the altar of the LORD" (1 Kgs 8:22). Later Solomon is portrayed as kneeling before the Lord. Furthermore, Solomon repeatedly acknowledges the power, might, glory, and great name of God (8:23, 42, 43). Such humility in the genre of prayer counters the narcissistic talk that we hear in much contemporary political discourse.

It is intriguing to note that Solomon, who shows a great deal of humility before God, urges God to "do according to all that the foreigner calls to you" (8:43). No qualifications are put forth regarding the prayers of those foreigners. No limitations or restrictions are imposed on the pleas of those who are not part of the people of Israel. One might suggest that Solomon's intercessory prayer seeks to incorporate the foreigner under the religious conviction of Yahwism. This point might be supported by referring to how Solomon's discourse portrays the foreigner as one who "knows" and "fears" the name of YHWH (8:43). Yet in Solomon's prayer, the foreigner is not forced to pray or make pilgrimage in Jerusalem; rather, the foreigner has agency and chooses to pray to YHWH.

This text of inclusion of the foreigner who fears YHWH is not alone in the Hebrew Bible. Isaiah 56:6–8 also speaks of foreigners as joining into the covenant of YHWH with Israel. Along with Solomon's intercession in behalf of the stranger (*nokhri*) or non-Israelite, the affirming and inclusive message of Isaiah 56 seems to be a counter perspective to nationalistic politics that seek to exclude foreigners from approaching the holy mountain:

> And the foreigners who join themselves to the LORD,
>> to minister to him, to love the name of the LORD,
>> and to be his servants,
> all who keep the sabbath, and do not profane it,
>> and hold fast my covenant—
> these I will bring to my holy mountain,
>> and make them joyful in my house of prayer;
> their burnt offerings and their sacrifices
>> will be accepted on my altar;
> for my house shall be called a house of prayer
>> for all peoples.
> Thus says the Lord GOD,
>> who gathers the outcasts of Israel,
> I will gather others to them
>> besides those already gathered. (Isa 56:6–8)

Solomon's prayer in behalf of the stranger stresses the care that the community of faith shows to the stranger. It underlines an important characteristic of the community of faith, namely, that it is unselfish. It cares about others. This openness to the needs of the other is not captive to fear or jealousy. And it is not meant to take control of the other. This openness treats the other as a subject whose needs and pleas matter to the community of faith. Isaiah's vision of welcoming the stranger into the community of faith emphasizes that the doors of the community of faith are open to the other. Because of a long history of colonization and coercive proselytization, many Christians have become sensitive about sharing their faith openly with the "other," for fear that speaking about their faith could be interpreted as being part of a colonial program. What is evident in Solomon's prayer and in Isaiah is that there is no coercion. The stranger chooses to pray, to make pilgrimage, and to join the covenant community. The foreigner is acting as one who decides for him- or herself. Because the religious other is choosing to join the faith community, welcoming the religious other into the covenant community is, in this case, a sign of treating the person as an active agent.

Seeing Goodness in the Other

As we consider the witness of an intercultural church amid inter-religious encounters, Luke's story of the healing of the servant of the centurion (found in 7:1–10) offers us many insights. First, the story shows signs of how people who are divided by socioeconomic, political, and religious divisions overcome these barriers in order to attend to the need of an ill human being who is close to death. A Roman leader and the Jewish elders work together to bring healing to a human being who is "highly valued."

According to Luke, a centurion who enjoys authority and various privileges and rights has a slave who is described at the beginning of the story as being sick to the point of dying and also as valued highly by his master. Being valued (*entimos*) refers to being "distinguished" (Luke 14:8), "honored" (Phil 2:29), and "precious" (1 Pet 2:4, 6). In the example from 1 Peter, the word is used to describe Jesus the cornerstone, who, although rejected by people, is chosen and precious in God's sight. The centurion hears that Jesus has come to Capernaum, so he asks some Jewish leaders to plead with Jesus in his behalf and ask Jesus to heal the slave.

Applying that story to our situations today, when a crisis breaks out and threatens a group in the community, people must collaborate and not let their differences stand as a stumbling block to taking action. They must choose to work together to respond to challenges when they arise. The challenges can be met when human beings are valued regardless of their religious, cultural, or socioeconomic backgrounds. The well-being of the community can be restored when those who are in power use their privilege for the sake of the other. Change can happen when vulnerability is coupled with trust. The centurion shows vulnerability, not for his own sake, but for the sake of another. He does not let his prestige stand in the way. Rather, he trusts that the Jewish leaders will help him because there has been a history of fostering respect

> Working with others who are different culturally and religiously to bring healing to this world depends on building long-standing relationships of trust.

and mutuality. In other words, working with others who are different culturally and religiously to bring healing to this world depends on building long-standing relationships of trust.

Second, the story teaches us to see the goodness in the other who is different from us culturally, religiously, socially, and politically. The Jewish elders acknowledge how the centurion loves their community and has expressed his love by building a synagogue for them. The leaders say to Jesus, "He is worthy of having you do this for him, for he loves our people, and it is he who built our synagogue for us" (7:5). The centurion manifests his love in a practical way that reflects not only tolerance of the Jewish faith but also appreciation for the community that needs a synagogue. Not only does the centurion respect the Jewish community, he also sacrifices to meet their needs. What is intriguing here is that the Jewish leaders acknowledge the centurion's acts of kindness and point to them as a reason why Jesus should heal his slave. The centurion also trusts that goodness will come from the Jewish leaders he asks to intercede for him with Jesus. And he trusts that Jesus will show compassion to him and his slave.

Although the centurion has done many good things for the Jewish community, and although the Jewish leaders say to Jesus that this man is "worthy," the centurion does not brag about his good deeds or piety. Instead, when Jesus arrives in Capernaum, the centurion creates space for Jesus to exercise his authority. He says,

"Lord, do not trouble yourself, for I am not worthy
to have you come under my roof; therefore I did not

presume to come to you. But only speak the word, and let my servant be healed. For I also am a man set under authority, with soldiers under me; and I say to one, 'Go,' and he goes, and to another, 'Come,' and he comes, and to my slave, 'Do this,' and the slave does it." When Jesus heard this he was amazed at him, and . . . he said, "I tell you, not even in Israel have I found such faith." (7:6–9)

The acknowledgment of the goodness in the other is expressed by Jesus, who declares that he has not seen faith within Israel like the faith of the centurion. This is a rare occasion in which even Jesus is amazed by someone's faith; usually people are amazed at what Jesus says or by the miracles that Jesus performs (Luke 11:14; 20:26). Here it is Jesus who is impressed with a stranger's faith. As an insider, Jesus goes even further to say that the outsider's faith is unmatched among God's people. This mutual recognition of the goodness within the other allows for an authentic ecounter between those who are different. In addition, it leads to the healing of a human being who is valued deeply by all of those in the encounter who are different from one another.

Mutual Need and Mutual Contribution in an Interreligious Setting

Various matrices of cross-cultural relations are embedded in the story of Joseph in Genesis 37–50. These include assimilation (Joseph's dress code, language, and marriage), separation (living in Goshen), and transnationality (moving between Egypt and

Canaan and funeral rituals for the deceased Jacob). But the story also brings to the fore many significant aspects of working with others who believe differently. Joseph the Hebrew and Pharaoh the Egyptian are different not just ethnically but also religiously. Despite their differences, they work together to prepare for the impending famine. In their exchange in Genesis 41, a common religious grounding plays a significant role in bringing them to see each other as active agents who can contribute to the well-being of the other. Joseph attributes Pharaoh's dreams to God, and Pharaoh says to his servants, "Can we find anyone else like this—one in whom is the spirit of God?" (Gen 41:38). Their faith focuses on what is common, and it does not exclude faith in God or the gifts that God has given for the sake of cooperation. Common ground is created in which faith plays a significant role in working interculturally.

When Pharaoh has disturbing dreams, and his officials fail to interpret the dreams for him, the chief cupbearer remembers Joseph, the Hebrew slave who is capable of interpreting dreams. Although he is imprisoned, the forced migrant Joseph is rushed to meet the most powerful man in Egypt. Still, Joseph takes the time to shave and change his garment, a sign of exercising his power of agency (41:14). Despite the difference in power between Pharaoh and Joseph, the text of Genesis 41 makes it clear that the need is mutual and that both parties, the migrant and the host, see each other as equal partners in facing the impending disaster of the famine. Pharaoh needs Joseph to interpret the dream for him, and Joseph needs Pharaoh to reexamine Joseph's unjust imprisonment. Pharaoh's need for Joseph is highlighted by the repetition of the phrase "and there is no one who can interpret it" (41:15–24). The solution to Pharaoh's anxiety lies with this Hebrew slave, who is gifted in interpreting dreams. Joseph also needs Pharaoh. We recall the last words Joseph said to the chief cupbearer upon his release from the prison: "But remember me when it is well with you; please do me the kindness to make mention of me to Pharaoh, and so get me out of this place" (Gen 40:14). Pharaoh needs Joseph to interpret the dream for him, and Joseph has the ability to meet Pharaoh's needs. Joseph needs Pharaoh to use his power to release him from prison, and Pharaoh can do that.

In addition to their mutual need and reciprocal contributions, this episode underscores another important aspect of the migrant-host relationship that would put the church, if it paid attention, on solid ground to become an intercultural church. Joseph and Pharaoh see each other as more than persons who can offer something that is needed. Joseph and Pharaoh both see each other as channels through which the divine communicates with humans. Joseph's interpretation of the dream begins and ends with a significant assertion, namely, that God has revealed what God is about to do to Pharaoh. In other words, these dreams are nothing but a revelation from God. Joseph recognizes the foreign king as a medium of divine revelation. The same is asserted in the middle of the interpretation, where Joseph reaffirms that God has shown Pharaoh what God is planning to do (40:25, 28, 32).

In his interpretation of the dream, Joseph declares to the king that "God has shown [*rah*] Pharaoh what God is about to do"

(41:28). And after he finishes interpreting the dream, he advises Pharaoh to "see" (*rah*), that is, to find a man of understanding and wisdom (41:33). The work of "showing" Pharaoh, which God has started through the dreams, Joseph brings to completion through his interpretation and wisdom. The next thing that Joseph offers Pharaoh as advice is to act (*'sh*). In Genesis 41:25, 32, the text speaks of God doing or God acting (*Elohim 'oseh*), and in 41:34, Pharaoh is acting in response to God's actions. Joseph continues the work of God by interpreting the dream and by offering wisdom to Pharaoh, while Pharaoh continues God's work through his actions.

Though Pharaoh now knows what the dreams mean and what must be done to deal with the impending famine, he expresses his need for Joseph this time not out of desperation but out of admiration. Pharaoh declares that God's Spirit is with Joseph in a remarkable way (41:38). Pharaoh goes on to speak of Joseph's qualifications: "Since God has shown you all this, there is no one so discerning and wise as you" (41:39). Three qualifications that Pharaoh's words highlight are understanding, wisdom, and knowledge. These three qualifications are not the result of wisdom schooling; they are the result of the work of the Spirit of God in Joseph (similar to the description of Bezalel in Exod 31:3). Knowledge, understanding, and wisdom are direct gifts that God has bestowed upon the migrant Joseph in the process of revealing God's intentions for what will happen in Egypt in the years to come. Pharaoh sees the Hebrew slave as a channel through which God reveals God's will. Joseph, in turn, signifies that he understands Pharaoh's dreams as coming from God when he says, "God has shown to Pharaoh what he is about to do" (Gen 41:28) and "Since God has shown you all this" (41:39).

It is noteworthy that Joseph and Pharaoh see each other not only as partners in facing the famine but also as channels through which God communicates future divine actions. Reinhard Achenbach notes, "The narrator of the Hebrew novelette does not claim to give a historical portrait of the Pharaoh's religion. Instead, in his perspective the Pharaoh can only act in the horizon of Elohim, the universal and unique God of Israel."[14] The story of Joseph does not, however, portray Elohim as "the unique God of Israel." Instead, given that both Joseph and the foreign king use the generic word *Elohim*, the narrative seems to obscure who God is. The text does not speak of an Egyptian God or an Israelite God but of a universal God. It is noteworthy that throughout Genesis 37–50, only the narrator uses the name of the Hebrew God, YHWH (LORD; Genesis 39). The rest of the characters, Hebrew and Egyptian, use the divine epithet "Elohim" (God). While Joseph refers to "God" when he named his children (Gen 41:50–52), he seems to have appropriated some of the religious practices in Egypt, including divination (44:5, 15). The story stands in contrast to Daniel 1–6, another diaspora narrative, which emphasizes isolation from the surrounding culture and highlights a contrast between the God of the Hebrews and the gods of the Babylonians (Dan 1:8–16; 2:28, 47).

To summarize what intercultural churches can learn from the Joseph story:

1. There is a mutual need. Pharaoh needs Joseph to interpret the dreams and to suggest a plan to face the famine; Joseph's words to the chief cupbearer express his need for Pharaoh to take notice of the injustice he has endured in prison (Gen 40:15).

2. Each of the parties involved in the cross-cultural transaction recognizes the other as a medium through which God reveals divine intentions for the world. Joseph considers Pharaoh's dream a divine revelation, and Pharaoh considers Joseph's interpretation and plans a result of divine illumination. Each of them contributes something significant to the process of facing the impending disaster, and more important, each receives this contribution as a divine gift.

Relationships in the church will be transformed when each member recognizes their need for the other but also when they become willing to offer their gifts in service to the other. For the church and society to become places where people from different cultural, religious, racial, and ethnic backgrounds can be equally welcomed and serve God and the world together, there has to be a sense of mutual need and reciprocal contribution. Sometimes recent migrants forget that they have something to offer, and host or settled communities forget that they are in need of and should remain open to receive what others can offer. Host communities are often framed as the side that offers hospitality, while the migrant communities are framed as the ones who receive what is offered. In this episode of the story of Joseph, we learn that host and migrant work together, despite their religious difference, by creating a common ground of giving and receiving.

Religious Freedom

Being grounded in one's faith is not antithetical to openness to the inclusion of the religious other, nor should it stand in contrast to seeing goodness in the other. Some biblical texts see religious otherness as a threat (Joshua 23), and other texts are skeptical of the deities of others (Isaiah 40–55). The basic point in these texts is a criticism of the people of Israel for not solely trusting in their own God. Still other biblical texts, however, allow for the coexistence of different beliefs. One of these texts is Micah 4:1–5.

> Being grounded in one's faith is not antithetical to openness for the inclusion of the religious other.

The vision in Micah 4:1–5 parallels the vision found in Isaiah 2:1–5. In this vision, the mountain of the Lord becomes the center of the earth, and all the peoples and the nations march to it, seeking the torah (teachings) of the Lord. Again, the people are not forced to go to the mountain of the Lord, for they say, "Come, let us go up to the mountain of the Lord" (Mic 4:2). The cohortative mood (expressing the speakers' desire) of the verb "let us go up" (*n'lh*) underlines their agency. When the Lord brings about justice between the nations,

> they shall beat their swords into plowshares,
> and their spears into pruning hooks;
> nation shall not lift up sword against nation,
> neither shall they learn war any more. (4:3)

When justice reigns and violence and war cease, peace and security will be enjoyed by everyone:

> They shall all sit under their own vines and under their
>   own fig trees,
>   and no one shall make them afraid. (4:4)

While Isaiah 2:5 reads,

> O house of Jacob,
>   come, let us walk
>   in the light of the Lord,

Micah 4:5 reads,

> For all the peoples walk,
>   each in the name of its god,
> but we will walk in the name of the Lord our God
>   forever and ever.

The difference between Isaiah and Micah is telling. Isaiah calls upon the people to recommit themselves to their God because they have abandoned their God by worshipping other gods (Isa 2:8). Micah calls the people to renew their commitment to their God while allowing other nations the freedom to worship their own gods. According to Micah 4:5, peace and security do not result from making all peoples one and the same; rather, these blessings result from doing justice, putting an end to violent wars, and making space for true pluralism, in which people are grounded in their own faith but do not impose it on others.

A Balanced Perspective on
Interreligious Encounters

Bearing these texts in mind, I return to the challenge I named earlier: how to be grounded in one's own faith while showing love, respect, and mutuality to others who hold other beliefs. I offer these general remarks with the belief that interreligious and ecumenical dialogues will be enriched when these conditions are in place:

- All parties are treated as equal subjects, that is, they speak for themselves and about their own faith.
- All parties articulate what makes them grounded in their own faith tradition and in the contributions their faith tradition makes to the theological conversation.
- All parties practice self-criticism regarding the way they articulate their own faith and the way they understand the other's faith (historical and contemporary encounters).
- All parties articulate what they might learn from the other tradition and what they might continue to ponder in their own and in the other's faith tradition.
- All parties open their hands, hearts, and minds to receive the gifts of the other, finding ways to serve one another and with one another.

When adherents of different faiths take seriously their own faith and the faith of the other, and when they find healthy ways of crossing boundaries and maintaining boundaries, they turn their differences into a source of theological enrichment, and they join together in bringing healing, well-being, and peace to our broken world.

Discussion Questions

1. On p. 172, the author states, "When the church becomes intercultural, it does not just preach reconciliation to the world, it lives it and it lets God's reconciling mission in the world permeate everything it does." What is your reaction to this statement? How does being an intercultural church intersect with being a "missional church"?

2. The author describes Martin Walton's model of pastoral care, which addresses the experiences of loss and ambivalence that surround migrants, refugees, and asylum seekers. In this model, pastoral care evolves along three dimensions: space ("Where am I?"), time ("When am I?"), and transcendence ("From where to where am I?"). How are these questions important both for the migrant or refugee and for the church seeking to be an intercultural church?

3. Review the description of Daniel Schipani's diagram of five possible cross-cultural orientations characterizing the relationship between migrant and host communities: accommodation, separation, segregation, assimilation, and integration (see pp. 181–82). Discuss what these orientations mean. As you reflect on your own faith community, which of these orientations best describes you? Why?

4. The author speaks of the importance of being grounded in one's own Christian faith while being open to the religious "other." What does this mean to you?

5. Read again the vision of the prophet Isaiah in 56:6–8 (see p. 188). What, if anything, does this text say to you about how established churches might view newcomers?

6. The author concludes the chapter with five specific conditions for interreligious and ecumenical dialogue. Review these statements and discuss them. Are any particularly difficult? If so, why? Which statement particularly resonates with you? Why?

ACKNOWLEDGMENTS

My reflections on what it means to be a church in an age of migration and in a society that is becoming more and more diverse began when I served as a pastor of an Arabic immigrant church in Jersey City in 2010–11. The first and second generations of this beloved congregation have taught me a lot about the possibilities and challenges that lie ahead of the church as a community of migrants and sojourners who live in the midst of a myriad of cultures. The idea of writing a book on intercultural church emerged in the summer of 2016 when I delivered the keynote address at the general assembly of the Mennonite Church Canada. I am grateful for the opportunity I had to interact with pastors and church members during this assembly in Saskatoon, Saskatchewan. My reflections on migration and the life of the church were deepened by many stimulating conversations with my colleagues Rachel Miller Jacobs, Daniel Schipani, Mary Schertz, Rebecca Slough, and Barbara Nelson Gingerich during the 2016–17 Scribes for the Reign of God seminar at Anabaptist Mennonite Biblical Seminary (AMBS). I am thankful for my students Peter Anderson, Grant Miller, Patrick Obonde, and Brian O'Leary, who interacted with some of the insights that I develop in this book as part of the Spring 2018 course Biblical Understandings of Migration that I taught at AMBS. Many thanks to Eleanor Kreider for giving me the permission to include the "Gathering around the Table" liturgy and to James Gingerich for helping with formatting the text and the music of the ritual. The manuscript of this book has improved as a result of the many helpful editorial suggestions of Scott Tunseth and Karen Schenkenfelder of Fortress Press. Many thanks to the editorial board of *Word & World* for accepting this book to be part of the series, and many thanks to Layne Johnson and many others at Fortress Press for their work on the production of the book. Special thanks go to Barbara Nelson Gingerich and to Peter Altmann for reading through a draft of this book and for offering many valuable editorial suggestions. All mistakes that remain are mine, of course.

Finally, I am indebted to my beloved partner, Carolin Marzouk, and our dear children, Calista and Julian, for their continuous love and support and for the wisdom they impart to me every day on how to live and thrive in liminal spaces between cultures. May this book inspire the church to form congregations in which people who are different culturally, racially, and ethnically worship, fellowship, and serve together for God's glory and for the good of the world.

A NARRATIVE OF THE LITURGY OF "GATHERING AROUND THE TABLE"

This table liturgy was developed by Alan and Eleanor Kreider. The liturgy has taken a life of its own, and it has been used and modified by various Christian groups and communities who shared weekly meals at churches or homes. This current version was edited and modified by James and Barbara Nelson Gingerich. The following is an account provided by Eleanor Kreider describing the genesis of the liturgy:

> In the mid-1990s a table group in Oxford met weekly for shared meals in each others' homes. The eight adults and three children were friends drawn from several Christian denominations. During a weekend retreat, the idea was born to shape a liturgy around the weekly shared meal. A first draft emerged; much of it stuck and remains as the bones of the liturgy. An early question was how strongly to cast it as a eucharistic service, based on the Institution Narrative. So that the children could participate fully, a subsequent version used Johannine texts and ceremonial water and bread. The first version included dishwashing

and the kitchen cleanup. One distinctive element of the table liturgy is its dispersed leadership. No one is designated beforehand to read particular "leader" sections. The table liturgy now appears in various countries, in each place taking on editorial changes to suit the characteristic language, culture, and circumstances. The first editorial group specifically indicated that others should use this liturgy freely, to augment and alter it to fit their circumstances.

—Eleanor Kreider, member of the original table group

Gathering around the Table

Words in bold italic type are said together. All other sentences can be led by anyone present.

The welcome

Jesus said "Listen, I am standing at the door and knocking: if you hear my voice and open the door, I will come in and eat with you, and you with me." ***We give thanks for this promise and for God's presence here with us.***

God wel - comes all, stran - gers and friends;

God's love is strong and it nev - er ends.

By John L. Bell

God welcomes us and so we greet one another:
[Name], ***we welcome you to this table in the name of Christ.***
Reply: Amen. It's good to be here.

Jesus said "When you have supper, do not invite just your friends, or relatives, or those who are wealthy … but rather invite the poor and the marginalized."

We confess to God the ways we have not been inclusive and welcoming in this past week. (*Pause*)

For our blindness to the needs of others, and our preoccupation with our own agenda,

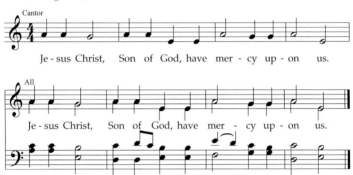

Je - sus Christ, Son of God, have mer - cy up - on us.

Je - sus Christ, Son of God, have mer - cy up - on us.

For our failure to pay attention to the still small voice in our lives,
Sung response: Jesus Christ, Son of God . . .

For our life choices this week that have not contributed to great love and justice in the world,
Sung response: Jesus Christ, Son of God . . .

The Promise of New Beginnings

The prophet Isaiah writes: On this mountain the Lord Almighty will prepare for all peoples a feast of rich food, a banquet of well-aged wines—the best of meats and the finest of wines. God will destroy on this mountain the shroud that is cast over all peoples, the sheet that covers all nations; God will swallow up death forever. Then the Lord will wipe away the tears from all faces, and take away the disgrace of the people from all the earth, for the Lord has spoken. In that day they will say,

This is our God, the one in whom we trusted, the one who saved us. This is the Lord for whom we waited; let us rejoice and be glad.

Bread and wine are placed on the table.

While they were at the table Jesus took a loaf of bread and after giving thanks, he broke it and gave it to them, saying, "Each time you eat this, remember me." Then he took a cup of wine, and gave it to them. "Each time you drink this, remember me."

Thank you, God, that ordinary things can become special when placed in your hands. Thank you that what is broken may be made whole and what is given is not wasted.

In the silence we think about where we experience brokenness and long for wholeness.

Bread is passed around. When all are served:

Be grateful when you touch bread.
Let it not lie uncared for, unwanted.
There is so much beauty in bread,
beauty of sun and soil, beauty of patient toil.
Winds and rain have caressed it;
Christ often blessed it.
Be grateful when you touch bread.

We eat bread together.

Wine is poured. When all are served:

Be loving when you drink wine.
Let its color, life, and joy be appreciated.
There is so much beauty in wine,
beauty of self-giving, beauty of forgiving.
Winds and rain have caressed it;
Christ often blessed it.
Be loving when you drink wine.

We drink together.

Let's say together …
Thank you, God, for love, for food, and for friends to share with.

Praise God for love, praise God for life, in age or youth, in calm or strife. Lift up your hearts! Let love be fed through death and life in bro-ken bread. A-men.

The first course is served.

Thank you, Lord, for this meal.
But we cannot live by bread alone.
We have shared it together
because we need each other.

[Name], we need you.
Reply: And I need you.

Lord God, as we bring our prayers,
we thank you that we can share in your kingdom
of justice and peace.
We come in our poverty, not in our wealth,
in our blindness, not with great faith,

in our weakness, not in our strength.
You welcome all people.
So now we bring to you those who need love, light and peace.

Night lights may be lit as we name individuals or situations.
After each candle is lit, we sing

Lord, in your mer - cy, hear our prayer!

Music: John L. Bell
Copyright © 1995, 1998 WGRG, Iona Community, Scotland.
GIA Publications, Inc., exclusive North American agent. All rights reserved. Used with permission.

Prayer for a New Earth

God of all places and this place: You promised a new earth
where the hungry will feast and the oppressed go free.
Come, Lord, build that place among us.

God of all times and this time: You promised a new day
when the fearful will laugh and the sick find healing.
Come, Lord, speed that time among us.

God of all people, our God: Take what we have and what we hope for
to make this a world where all people find good news.
We come, Lord, to share in the work of your kingdom,
until the new earth is created among us. Amen.

Heav-en and earth, join to wor-ship your Cre-a-tor!
Heav-en and earth, join to wor - - - ship.

Sing to the Lord, praise the One from whom you came.
Sing to the Lord from whom you came.

Sing a new song to the God who goes be-fore us,
Sing a new song to the God be - fore us,

(Hum)

ma-king all new, leav - ing no-bo-dy the same.
ma-king all new, leav - ing none the same.

Dessert is served.

It is evening and night is drawing near. The night is for stillness.
Let us be still in the presence of God.

It is evening after a long day.
What has been done has been done.
What has not been done has not been done.
Let it be.

The night is dark.
Let our fears of the darkness of the world and of our lives rest in you.

The night is quiet.
Let the quietness of your peace enfold us, all dear to us, and all who have no peace.

2 Darkness soon will come . . .
3 See your children, Lord . . .
4 We are with you, Lord . . .
5 Keep us in your love . . .
6 Soon we go to rest . . .
7 Night is falling . . .

The night heralds the dawn.
Let us look expectantly to a new day, new joys, new possibilities.
Amen.

2 With love our hearts are ablazing
for those who roam
and wander far away
though longing home.

3 Each day our friendship is growing
and with all speed
we share our bread and wine,
a hasty meal.

NOTES

CHAPTER 1: WHAT IS AN INTERCULTURAL CHURCH?

1. Paul S. Minear, *Images of the Church in the New Testament*, New Testament Library (Louisville: Westminster John Knox, 2004; orig. pub. 1960).
2. Agnes M. Brazal and Emmanuel S. De Guzman, *Intercultural Church: Bridge of Solidarity in the Migration Context* (n.p.: Borderless, 2015), 47–48.
3. Grace Ji-Sun Kim and Jann Aldredge-Clanton, eds., introduction to *Intercultural Ministry: Hope for a Changing World*, ed. (Valley Forge, PA: Judson, 2017), x.
4. Michell R. Hammer, "The Intercultural Development Inventory: An Approach to Assessing and Building Intercultural Competence," in *Contemporary Leadership and Intercultural Competence: Exploring the Cross-Cultural Dynamics within Organizations*, ed. Michael A. Moodian (Los Angeles: SAGE, 2009), 203–17.
5. M. R. Hammer, M. J. Bennett, and R. Wiseman, "The Intercultural Development Inventory: A Measure of Intercultural Sensitivity," *International Journal of Intercultural Relations* 27 (2003): 421–43.
6. John Calvin, *Institutes of the Christian Religion: A New Translation* (London: Clarke, 1962), 1.1.1–2.
7. Henri J. M. Nouwen, Ron P. van den Bosch, and Theo Robert, *With Open Hands* (Notre Dame, IN: Ave Maria, 1972), 114.

8. Richard I. Pervo and Harold W. Attridge, *Acts: A Commentary*, Hermeneia (Minneapolis: Fortress, 2009), 282.

9. Anthony B. Robinson and Robert W. Wall, *Called to Be Church: The Book of Acts for a New Day* (Grand Rapids: Eerdmans, 2006), 158.

10. Eric D. Barreto, "A Gospel on the Move: Practice, Proclamation, and Place in Luke-Acts," *Interpretation* 72, no. 2 (April 2018): 184–85.

11. Joel B. Green, *Conversion in Luke-Acts: Divine Action, Human Cognition, and the People of God* (Grand Rapids: Baker Academic, 2015), 163.

12. Mary Douglas, *Purity and Danger: An Analysis of Concepts of Pollution and Taboo* (Middlesex: Penguin, 1970), 51–71.

13. Jacob Milgrom, *Leviticus: A Book of Ritual and Ethics*, Continental Commentaries (Minneapolis: Fortress, 2004).

14. David M. Freidenreich, *Foreigners and Their Food: Constructing Otherness in Jewish, Christian, and Islamic Law* (Berkeley: University of California Press, 2011).

15. J. Bradley Chance, *Acts*, Smyth & Helwys Bible Commentary (Macon, GA: Smyth & Helwys, 2007), 163.

CHAPTER 2: STRANGERS OURSELVES: READING THE BIBLE AS SOJOURNERS

1. Claus Westermann, *Genesis 1–36: A Commentary* (Minneapolis: Augsburg, 1985), 373.

2. Elisabeth Robertson Kennedy, *Seeking a Homeland: Sojourn and Ethnic Identity in the Ancestral Narratives of Genesis*, Biblical Interpretation Series 106 (Boston: Brill, 2011), 108.

3. For a full discussion of the implications of this narrative for a theology of migration and peace building, see Safwat Marzouk, "Famine, Migration, and Conflict: The Way of Peace; A Reading of Genesis 26," in *Where Are We? Pastoral Environments and Care for Migrants; Intercultural and Interreligious Perspectives*, ed. Daniel S. Schipani, Martin Walton, and Dominiek Lootens (Düsseldorf: Society for Intercultural Pastoral Care and Counseling, 2018), 3–18.

4. José E. Ramírez Kidd, *Alterity and Identity in Israel: The* rg *in the Old Testament*, rev. ed. (1999; repr., New York: De Gruyter, 2012), 132.

5. John Hall Elliott, *A Home for the Homeless: A Sociological Exegesis of 1 Peter, Its Situation and Strategy* (Philadelphia: Fortress, 1981).

6. Reinhard Feldmeier, *Die Christen als Fremde: Die Metapher der Fremde in der antiken Welt, im Urchristentum und im 1. Petrusbrief* [Christians as Strangers: The Metaphor of the Stranger in the Ancient World, in Early Christianity and in 1 Peter] (Tübingen: Mohr, 1992).

7. Benjamin H. Dunning, *Aliens and Sojourners: Self as Other in Early Christianity* (Philadelphia: University of Pennsylvania Press, 2009), 12.

8. The Septuagint is the earliest Greek translation of the Hebrew Bible (the Old Testament).

9. Shively T. J. Smith, *Strangers to Family: Diaspora and 1 Peter's Invention of God's Household* (Waco: Baylor University Press, 2016), 166.

10. Stanley Hauerwas and William H. Willimon, *Resident Aliens: Life in the Christian Colony*, 25th anniv. ed. (Nashville: Abingdon, 2014), 48.

11. Walter Brueggemann, "Alien Witness: How God's People Challenge Empire," *Christian Century*, March 6, 2007, 28–32.

12. Amy Coplan and Peter Goldie, *Empathy: Philosophical and Psychological Perspectives* (Oxford: Oxford University Press, 2011), 4.

13. Coplan and Goldie, *Empathy*, 6.

14. Coplan and Goldie, *Empathy*, 7.

15. Coplan and Goldie, *Empathy*, 9.

16. Coplan and Goldie, *Empathy*, 15–16.

CHAPTER 3: WORSHIP AND THE INTERCULTURAL REALITY OF THE CHURCH

1. Thomas H. Schattauer, *Inside Out: Worship in an Age of Mission* (Minneapolis: Fortress, 1999), 3.

2. Brevard S. Childs, *The Book of Exodus: A Critical, Theological Commentary* (Philadelphia: Westminster, 1974), 57.

3. Childs, *Book of Exodus*, 56.

4. Mitchell G. Reddish, *Revelation*, Smyth & Helwys Bible Commentary (Macon, GA: Smyth & Helwys, 2005), 92.

5. Reddish, *Revelation*, 92.

6. Loren L. Johns, *Lamb Christology of the Apocalypse of John: An Investigation into Its Origins and Rhetorical Force* (Eugene, OR: Wipf & Stock, 2014), 170.

7. Steven J. Friesen, *Imperial Cults and the Apocalypse of John: Reading Revelation in the Ruins* (Oxford: Oxford University Press, 2001), 200.

8. Reddish, *Revelation*, 110.

9. Jean Zizioulas and Paul McPartlan, *Communion and Otherness: Further Studies in Personhood and the Church* (London: T&T Clark, 2006), 4–5.

10. Zizioulas and McPartlan, *Communion and Otherness,* 5–6.

11. Reddish, *Revelation*, 104.

12. Elisabeth Schüssler Fiorenza, *Revelation: Vision of a Just World*, Proclamation Commentaries (Minneapolis: Fortress, 1991), 61.

13. Friesen, *Imperial Cults and the Apocalypse of John*, 182.

14. Justo L. González, *For the Healing of the Nations: The Book of Revelation in an Age of Cultural Conflict* (Maryknoll, NY: Orbis, 1999). González notes that diversity is not only a marker of the people of the kingdom of God; diversity in language, ethnicity, and cultural background happen also among those who follow the beast (e.g., Rev 11:9).

15. David E. Aune, *Revelation 1–5*, Word Biblical Commentary 52a (Dallas: Word, 1997), 361. Other passages in Revelation that seek to reflect this universality include Rev 7:9; 10:11; 11:9; 13:7; 14:6; 17:15 (cf. Isa 66:18; Zech 8:22).

16. Aune, *Revelation 1–5*, 362.

17. Sandra Maria Van Opstal, *The Next Worship: Glorifying God in a Diverse World* (Downers Grove, IL: IVP Books, 2016).

18. "Nairobi Statement on Worship and Culture Full Text," Calvin Institute of Christian Worship, June 16, 2014, https://tinyurl.com/yb6ehzbe.

19. Anne Zaki, "Shall We Dance? Reflections on the Nairobi Statement on Worship and Culture," in *Worship and Mission for the Global Church: An Ethnodoxology Handbook*, ed. James R. Krabill, Frank Fortunato, Robin P Harris, and Brian Schrag (Pasadena, CA: William Carey Library, 2013), 79.

20. Zaki, "Shall We Dance?" 79.

21. Zaki, "Shall We Dance?" 79.

22. Aune, *Revelation 1–5*, 359.

23. Carol Doran and Thomas H. Troeger, *Trouble at the Table: Gathering the Tribes for Worship* (Nashville: Abingdon, 1992), 26.

24. Doran and Troeger, *Trouble at the Table*, 37.

25. Doran and Troeger, *Trouble at the Table*, 37–38.

26. Friesen, *Imperial Cults and the Apocalypse of John*, 196.

27. Reddish, *Revelation*, 97.

28. Kathy Black, *Culturally-Conscious Worship* (St. Louis: Chalice, 2000), 107.

29. Black, *Culturally-Conscious Worship*, 108.

30. Brian K. Blount, *Revelation: A Commentary*, New Testament Library (Louisville: Westminster John Knox, 2009), 133.

31. Reddish, *Revelation*, 104.

32. Kathleen M. O'Connor, *Lamentations and the Tears of the World* (Maryknoll, NY: Orbis, 2002), 128.

33. Walter Brueggemann, "The Costly Loss of Lament," *Journal for the Study of the Old Testament* 36 (1986): 57–71.

34. W. Derek Suderman, "The Cost of Losing Lament for the Community of Faith: On Brueggemann, Ecclesiology, and the Social Audience of Prayer," *Journal of Theological Interpretation* 6, no. 2 (2012): 201–17.

35. William Blaine-Wallace, "The Politics of Tears: Lamentation as Justice-Making," in *Injustice and the Care of Souls: Taking Oppression Seriously in Pastoral Care*, ed. Sheryl A.

Kujawa-Holbrook and Karen Brown Montagno (Minneapolis: Fortress, 2009), 188.

36. Reddish, *Revelation*, 148.

CHAPTER 4: BABEL AND PENTECOST: MOVING FROM BEING MONOCULTURAL TO INTERCULTURAL

1. Michael Pasquale and Nathan L. K. Bierma, *Every Tribe and Tongue: A Biblical Vision for Language in Society* (Eugene, OR: Pickwick, 2011), 1.

2. Sandra Maria Van Opstal, *The Next Worship: Glorifying God in a Diverse World* (Downers Grove, IL: IVP Books, 2016), 19.

3. Augustine of Hippo, *The Homilies on John*, ed. James Innes and John Gibb, extended annotated ed. (Altenmünster: Jazzybee, 2012).

4. Theodore Hiebert, "The Tower of Babel and the Origin of the World's Cultures," *Journal of Biblical Literature* 126, no. 1 (2007): 40.

5. Ched Myers and Matthew Colwell, *Our God Is Undocumented: Biblical Faith and Immigrant Justice* (Maryknoll, NY: Orbis, 2012), 23.

6. Myers and Colwell, *Our God Is Undocumented*, 25.

7. Myers and Colwell, *Our God Is Undocumented*, 26.

8. Myers and Colwell, *Our God Is Undocumented*, 27.

9. Myers and Colwell, *Our God Is Undocumented*, 27.

10. Eleazar S. Fernandez, "Diaspora, Babel, Pentecost, and the Strangers in Our Midst: Birthing a Church of Radical Hospitality," in *Postcolonial Interventions: Essays in Honor of R. S. Sugirtharajah*, The Bible in the Modern World, ed. Tat-siong Benny Liew and R. S. Sugirtharajah (Sheffield: Sheffield Phoenix, 2009), 149.

11. Hiebert, "Tower of Babel," 31.

12. Hiebert, "Tower of Babel," 35.

13. Hiebert, "Tower of Babel," 46.

14. Hiebert, "Tower of Babel," 50.

15. Beverly Roberts Gaventa, *The Acts of the Apostles*, Abingdon New Testament Commentaries (Nashville: Abingdon, 2003), 75.

16. John Calvin, *Commentaries on the First Book of Moses Called Genesis*, trans. John King (Grand Rapids: Baker, 1979), 331.
17. William H. Willimon, *Acts*, Interpretation: A Bible Commentary for Teaching and Preaching (Atlanta: John Knox, 1988), 32.
18. David Smith and Barbara Maria Carvill, *The Gift of the Stranger: Faith, Hospitality, and Foreign Language Learning* (Grand Rapids: Eerdmans, 2000), 15.
19. Letty M. Russell, J. Shannon Clarkson, and Kate M. Ott, *Just Hospitality: God's Welcome in a World of Difference* (Louisville: Westminster John Knox, 2009), 61.
20. Fernandez, "Diaspora, Babel, Pentecost," 151.
21. Fernandez, "Diaspora, Babel, Pentecost," 151.
22. Soong-Chan Rah, *Many Colors: Cultural Intelligence for a Changing Church*, rev. ed. (Chicago: Moody, 2010), 88–89.
23. Duane Elmer, *Cross-Cultural Connections: Stepping Out and Fitting In around the World* (Downers Grove, IL: InterVarsity, 2002), 117–90.

CHAPTER 5: FOOD AND BUILDING AN INTERCULTURAL CHURCH

1. Cláudio Carvalhaes, *Eucharist and Globalization: Redrawing the Borders of Eucharistic Hospitality* (Eugene, OR: Pickwick, 2013), 267.
2. Panayotis Coutsoumpos, *Community, Conflict, and the Eucharist in Roman Corinth: The Social Setting of Paul's Letter* (Lanham, MD: University Press of America, 2006), 102.
3. George Hunsinger, *The Eucharist and Ecumenism: Let Us Keep the Feast*, Current Issues in Theology (New York: Cambridge University Press, 2008), 255.
4. Carvalhaes, *Eucharist and Globalization*, 266.
5. Massimo Montanari, *Food Is Culture*, Arts and Traditions of the Table (New York: Columbia University Press, 2006), 133.
6. Soong-Chan Rah, *Many Colors: Cultural Intelligence for a Changing Church* (Chicago: Moody, 2010), 58.

7. Katharine Doob Sakenfeld, *Ruth*, Interpretation: A Bible Commentary for Teaching and Preaching (Louisville: John Knox, 1999), 39.
8. Peter Altmann, "Everyday Meals for Extraordinary People: Eating and Assimilation in the Book of Ruth," in *Decisive Meals: Table Politics in Biblical Literature*, ed. Nathan MacDonald, Luzia Sutter Rehmann, and Kathy Ehrensperger, Library of New Testament Studies 449 (London: T&T Clark, 2012).

CHAPTER 6: THE WITNESS OF THE INTERCULTURAL CHURCH

1. Lois Barrett, *Treasure in Clay Jars: Patterns in Missional Faithfulness*, The Gospel and Our Culture (Grand Rapids: Eerdmans, 2004), x.
2. Brenda Consuelo Ruiz, "Women and Migration in Central America: Pastoral Reflections," in *Where Are We? Pastoral Environments and Care for Migrants; Intercultural and Interreligious Perspectives,* ed. Daniel S. Schipani, Martin Walton, and Dominiek Lootens (Düsseldorf: Society for Intercultural Pastoral Care and Counseling, 2018), 123.
3. Martin Walton, "Recovering Context: Parameters of Pastoral Care with Migrants," in Schipani et al., *Where Are We?*, 172.
4. Walton, "Recovering Context," 174.
5. Walton, "Recovering Context," 176.
6. Gemma Tulud Cruz, *Toward a Theology of Migration: Social Justice and Religious Experience* (New York: Palgrave Macmillan, 2014), 127–40.
7. Cruz, *Toward a Theology of Migration*, 128–29.
8. Cruz, *Toward a Theology of Migration*, 129–34.
9. Cruz, *Toward a Theology of Migration*, 134–37.
10. Cruz, *Toward a Theology of Migration*, 137–40.
11. Daniel S. Schipani, "Faith Communities as Mediating Spaces," in Schipani et al., *Where Are We?*, 218.
12. Schipani, "Faith Communities as Mediating Spaces," 220.
13. Matthew Kaemingk, *Christian Hospitality and Muslim Immigration in an Age of Fear* (Grand Rapids: Eerdmans, 2018), 23.

14. Reinhard Achenbach, "How to Speak about GOD with Non-Israelites," in *The Post-Priestly Pentateuch: New Perspectives on Its Redactional Development and Theological Profiles*, ed. Federico Giuntoli and Konrad Schmid, FAT 101 (Tübingen: Mohr Siebeck, 2015), 45.

RECOMMENDED BOOKS ON THE TOPIC

Brazal, Agnes M., and Emmanuel S. de Guzman. *Intercultural Church: Bridge of Solidarity in the Migration Context*. N.p.: Borderless Press, 2015.

Carroll R., M. Daniel. *Christians at the Border: Immigration, the Church, and the Bible*. 2nd ed. Grand Rapids: Brazos Press, 2013.

Cruz, Gemma Tulud. *An Intercultural Theology of Migration*. Leiden: Brill, 2010.

———. *Toward a Theology of Migration: Social Justice and Religious Experience*. New York: Palgrave Macmillan, 2014.

Dunning, Benjamin H. *Aliens and Sojourners: Self as Other in Early Christianity*. Philadelphia: University of Pennsylvania Press, 2009.

Kaemingk, Matthew. *Christian Hospitality and Muslim Immigration in an Age of Fear*. Grand Rapids: Eerdmans, 2018.

Kim, Grace Ji-Sun, and Jann Aldredge-Clanton, eds. *Intercultural Ministry: Hope for a Changing World*. Valley Forge, PA: Judson Press, 2017.

McGill, Jenny. *Religious Identity and Cultural Negotiation: Toward a Theology of Christian Identity in Migration.* Eugene, OR: Pickwick, 2016.

Myers, Ched, and Matthew Colwell. *Our God Is Undocumented: Biblical Faith and Immigrant Justice.* Maryknoll, NY: Orbis, 2012.

Opstal, Sandra Maria Van. *The Next Worship: Glorifying God in a Diverse World.* Downers Grove, IL: IVP, 2016.

Rah, Soong-Chan. *Many Colors: Cultural Intelligence for a Changing Church.* Chicago: Moody, 2010.

Schipani, Daniel, Martin Walton, and Dominiek Lootens, eds. *Where Are We? Pastoral Environments and Care for Migrants, Intercultural and Interreligious Perspectives.* Düsseldorf: Society for Intercultural Pastoral Care and Counseling, 2018.

Snyder, Susanna. *Asylum-Seeking, Migration and Church.* Burlington, VT: Routledge, 2012.

Snyder, Susanna, Joshua Ralston, and Agnes M. Brazal, eds. *Church in an Age of Global Migration: A Moving Body.* New York: Palgrave Macmillan, 2016.

WORD & WORLD BOOKS

THEOLOGY FOR CHRISTIAN MINISTRY

Informing and inspiring Christian leaders and communities to proclaim God's *Word* to a *World* God created and loves. Articulating the fullness of both realities and the creative intersection between them.

Word & World Books is a partnership between Luther Seminary, the board of the periodical *Word & World*, and Fortress Press. Other books in the series include the following:

Future Faith: Ten Challenges Reshaping Christianity in the 21st Century by Wesley Granberg-Michaelson (978-1-5064-3344-8)

Liberating Youth from Adolescence by Jeremy Paul Myers (978-1-5064-3343-1)

Elders Rising: The Promise and Peril of Aging by Roland D. Martinson (978-1-5064-4054-5)

I Can Do No Other: The Church's New Here We Stand Moment by Anna M. Madsen (978-1-5064-2737-9)